# TEST
# YOUR WORD
# POWER

From the Ballantine Reference Library
*Published by Ballantine Books:*

NEW WORDS DICTIONARY
Harold LeMay, Sid Lerner, and Marian Taylor

1000 MOST CHALLENGING WORDS
Norman W. Schur

1000 MOST IMPORTANT WORDS
Norman W. Schur

PRACTICAL ENGLISH: 1,000 MOST EFFECTIVE
WORDS
Norman W. Schur

THE RANDOM HOUSE BASIC DICTIONARY
French-English-French
Edited by Francesca L.V. Langbaum

THE RANDOM HOUSE BASIC DICTIONARY
German-English-German
Edited by Jenni Karding Moulton

THE RANDOM HOUSE BASIC DICTIONARY
Italian-English-Italian
Edited by Robert A. Hall, Jr.

THE RANDOM HOUSE BASIC DICTIONARY
Spanish-English-Spanish
Edited by Donald F. Sola

THE RANDOM HOUSE BASIC DICTIONARY OF
SYNONYMS AND ANTONYMS
Edited by Laurence Urdang

THE RANDOM HOUSE DICTIONARY
Edited by Jess Stein

TEST YOUR WORD POWER
Jerome B. Agel

THE WORD-A-DAY VOCABULARY BUILDER
Berger Evans

# TEST YOUR WORD POWER

**THE BALLANTINE REFERENCE LIBRARY**

## JEROME B. AGEL

BALLANTINE BOOKS • NEW YORK

Sale of this book without a front cover may be unauthorized. If this book is coverless, it may have been reported to the publisher as "unsold or destroyed" and neither the author nor the publisher may have received payment for it.

Copyright © 1984 by Jerome B. Agel

All rights reserved under International and Pan-American Copyright Conventions. Published in the United States by Ballantine Books, a divison of Random House, Inc., New York, and simultaneously in Canada by Random House of Canada Limited, Toronto.

Library of Congress Catalog Card Number: 84-91049

ISBN 0-345-30897-2

Printed in Canada

First Edition: September 1984
Fourth Printing: September 1991

For many of the definitions, etymologies, and pronunciations, this book is indebted to THE RANDOM HOUSE DICTIONARY OF THE ENGLISH LANGUAGE, in particular to the Ballantine paperback edition.

J. A.

"A word is the skin of a living thought."
—Oliver Wendell Holmes

# Contents

vii

# Pronunciation Key

| SYMBOLS | KEY WORDS | SYMBOLS | KEY WORDS | SYMBOLS | KEY WORDS |
|---------|-----------|---------|-----------|---------|-----------|
| a | bat | n | now | û(r) | burn |
| ā | cape | ng | sing, sink | v | voice |
| â(r) | dare | ng·g | finger | w | west |
| ä | father | o | proper | y | yes |
| b | back | ō | no | z | zeal |
| ch | chief | ô | raw | zh | vision, |
| d | do | oi | joy | | mirage |
| e | set | ŏŏ | book | | |
| ē | seat | ōō | fool | UNACCENTED: | |
| ēr | ear | ou | loud | | |
| f | fit | p | pull | ə | alone, |
| g | good | r | read | | circus |
| h | hear | s | miss | ə | cradle |
| i | big | sh | shoe, | | (krād'əl) |
| ī | bite | | lotion | | redden |
| j | just | t | ten | | (red'ən) |
| k | keep | th | thin | | fire (fī'ər) |
| l | low, all | th | that | MAIN STRESS: ' | |
| m | mouth | u | up, love | WEAKER STRESS: ' | |

xiii

# Chapter I

## Vocabulary Test No. 1

Which word or phrase is nearest in meaning to each of the following headwords from the Constitution of the United States?

1. appropriate   (ə prō′prē it)
   (a) suitable for a purpose or use
   (b) notified
   (c) distributed proportionately
   (d) esteemed, cherished

2. insurrection   (in′sə rek′shan)
   (a) narrow-mindedness
   (b) essential part of the whole
   (c) outbreak against an established authority
   (d) reliance on intellect

3. tranquillity   (traṅgkwil′i tē)
   (a) enduring state of unagitated quietness
   (b) ordinary experience, thought, or belief
   (c) portent
   (d) state of lying across a bed while wrapped in a sheet

4. posterity   (po ster′ i tē)
   (a) bottom of the pile
   (b) all future generations collectively
   (c) publication after the death of the author
   (d) candidate for admission into a religious order

1

5. felony   (fel'ənē)
   (a) boggy land
   (b) circular rim or part of the rim of a wheel
   (c) seam on a flag
   (d) an offense that is graver than a misdemeanor

6. bounty   (boun'tē)
   (a) bunch of flowers for ceremonial use
   (b) generosity in giving
   (c) expurgation
   (d) limit or destination

7. quorum   (kwôr'əm)
   (a) something that formerly was
   (b) external angle of a wall
   (c) membership of any group that by law can carry handguns and muskets
   (d) the number of members of an organization required to be present to transact business legally

8. to abridge   (əbrij')
   (a) to abort
   (b) to shorten or condense
   (c) to pull (a tooth)
   (d) to cross (a river)

9. militia   (milish'ə)
   (a) emperor of Japan
   (b) signposts showing distance in miles to or from a place
   (c) citizens enrolled in military service but called only in emergencies
   (d) elected teenage men responsible for the safety of local womenfolk

10. to redress   (ridres')
   (a) to set right what is wrong
   (b) to put on again
   (c) to suggest or remind
   (d) to skirt an issue

**Correct answers:** 1 (a), 2 (c), 3 (a), 4 (b), 5 (d), 6 (b), 7 (d), 8 (b), 9 (c), 10 (a)

**Your score:** _____
(10 correct: superb; 9–7 correct: good; 6–5 correct: fair)

## False Impressions

Match the numbers at the left with the letters at the right.

1. "hangnail" does not hang but _____

2. "mushroom" is not a room in which we eat mush but _____

3. "outrage" does not contain the words "out" and "rage" but _____

4. "titmouse" is not a mouse with prominent breasts but _____

5. "scot-free" does not mean free like a Scotsman but _____

6. "mohair" is not related to "hair" but _____

7. "piggyback" was not invented by or for pigs but _____

8. "catgut" was not named for the gut of cats but _____

9. "forlorn hope" is not derived from "hope" but _____

10. "ear of corn" has nothing to do with an ear but _____

11. "Key West" neither is a key we put into a lock nor does it lie in the west but _____

(a) the first part of the term is related to the Latin word *acus*.

(b) actually means "choice."

(c) comes from a word referring to a choice of conveyance.

(d) is a single word coming from Medieval Latin.

(e) is derived from two unrelated old words.

(f) comes from a Latin word for "beyond," plus a common prefix.

(g) refers to something in the water and to invisible parts of our body.

(h) reflects the approximate pronunciation of a French word.

(i) is a word that expresses pain.

(j) has something to do with the tax collector.

(k) originally referred to losing one's way.

4

12. "crayfish" is not a fish and is not even derived from the word "fish" but _____

(l) has an origin that remains unexplained.

---

**Correct answers:**

1(i) Not a nail that hangs but one that causes *ang*, Old English for "pain."

2(d) From Middle English *muscheron*, from Old French *meisseron*, from Medieval Latin *mussirio*, all meaning "mushroom."

3(f) "Outr-" plus "-age": Old French *outrage*, from Latin *ultra*, "beyond," plus the prefix *-age*.

4(e) From *tit*, "small," and *mase*, an Old English word for our "titmouse," which is, of course, not a rodent but a bird. The folk etymology has been carried so far that the plural nowadays is "titmice," instead of the more appropriate "titmouses." (But note that "mongoose," from the Marathi word *mangus*, forms the etymologically correct plural "mongooses.")

5(j) From Middle English *scot*, "tax, fine."

6(b) From Italian *moccaiaro*, from Arabic *mukkayyar*, "choice."

7(c) From *pick-a-back* and *pick-a-pack*.

8(l) No one knows why cats are referred to when the animals whose intestines are used have always been sheep, and occasionally cattle. (But who knows whether "cattle gut" or "calves' gut" could have led to "catgut.")

9(k) From Dutch *verloren hoop*, "lost troop."

10(a) "Ear" comes from Old Frisian *ar*, akin to Dutch *aar* and German *Ähre*, and related to Latin *acus*, all meaning "husk" or "chaff."

11(g) "Key" was adapted from Spanish *cayo*, "small island," and "West" was adapted from Spanish *hueso*, "bone." "Key West," therefore, means "bone island."

**12(h)** From French *écrevisse*, from Germanic *krebiz*,
"crab." The French pronunciation (ākrevis') was
perhaps misheard as "crayfish."

Your score: _____
(12–11 correct: superb; 10–7 correct: good; 6–5 correct:
fair)

# Vocabulary Test No. 2

Which word or phrase is nearest in meaning to each of the following headwords from the musical comedy *Company*?

1. supercilious   (sōō′pərsil′ē·əs)
   (a) above the top living quarters of a ship
   (b) haughtily aloof
   (c) distributing light and shade in a picture
   (d) silly beyond description

2. trivia   (triv′ē·ə)
   (a) three-way road or highway without directional signs
   (b) matters or things of very slight importance
   (c) gossamer
   (d) triangular piece of material inserted in a stuffed shirt

3. to humiliate   (hyōōmil′ē·āt′)
   (a) to moisten
   (b) to put organic material in soils (produced by the decomposition of plants)
   (c) to hum a tune
   (d) to injure (someone's) self-respect, esp. in public

4. to writhe   (rīth)
   (a) to twist the body about, as in pain
   (b) to withhold
   (c) to surround
   (d) to bequeath

5. phenomenon   (finom′ənon′)
   (a) anything that is next to the last
   (b) boy wonder, esp. in matters of intimacy
   (c) fact, occurrence, or circumstance observed or observable
   (d) roofed structure at the door of a building for sheltering persons entering and leaving vehicles

7

6. **to misconstrue** (mis′kənstrōō′)
   (a) to be pigheaded
   (b) to misunderstand the meaning of (something)
   (c) to misrepresent
   (d) to match badly or unsuitably

7. **cliché** (klēshā′)
   (a) a boxer's arm lock around the other's waist
   (b) the science that deals with the state of language
   (c) trite, stereotyped expression
   (d) light, sharp, ringing sound

8. **exotic** (igzot′ik)
   (a) exaggerated
   (b) strikingly unusual or strange
   (c) out of step
   (d) snaring

9. **zombie** (zom′bē)
   (a) catatonic soul
   (b) (electronic) guitar developed for rock groups
   (c) flying fortress
   (d) corpse brought to life by a supernatural force

10. **bliss** (blis)
    (a) supreme happiness
    (b) ambidexterity
    (c) overwhelming all-out attack
    (d) balloon

---

**Correct answers:** 1 (b), 2 (b), 3 (d), 4 (a), 5 (c), 6 (b), 7 (c), 8 (b), 9 (d), 10 (a)

**Your score:** _____
(10 correct: superb; 9–7 correct: good; 6–5 correct: fair)

# Fill In the Blanks

Example:
uncompromising, as in politics:

i __ __ __ a __ s __ g __ __ __

The answer is "intransigent."

1. a ceremonial staff carried by a bishop or abbot:
   __ r o s __ e __

2. sincerely remorseful: __ o __ __ r __ t __

3. an intentional exaggeration not intended to be taken
   literally: __ y p __ __ b __ l e

4. sick from excessive drinking and eating:
   c r __ __ __ __ e __ t

5. salty or briny; distasteful or unpleasant:
   __ __ __ c k i s h

6. understood without being openly expressed; unvoiced
   or unspoken: __ __ __ i __

7. clever but specious argument:
   s __ p __ __ s __

8. the part of the leg between the knee and the ankle:
   __ __ a n k

9. a confused mixture or jumble: __ a r r a __ __

10. a person who eats excessively; a person with a great
    desire or capacity for something: g l u __ __ __ __

---

Correct answers: 1.crosier 2. contrite 3. hyperbole 4. crap-
ulent 5. brackish 6. tacit 7. sophism 8. shank 9. farrago 10.
glutton

Your score:_____
(10–9 correct: superb; 8–6 correct: good; 5–4 correct: fair)

# Vocabulary Test No. 3

Which word or phrase is nearest in meaning to each of the following headwords from J. D. Salinger's *The Catcher in the Rye*?

1. **phony** (fō′nē)
   (a) long-distance
   (b) resonant
   (c) not genuine or real
   (d) webless, as a baseball glove

2. **brassy** (bras′ē)
   (a) unpretentious
   (b) essential
   (c) impudent
   (d) spoiled

3. **hemorrhage** (hem′ərij)
   (a) profuse bleeding
   (b) one of the wounds of Christ on the Cross
   (c) painful enlargement of internal or external veins in the rectum
   (d) half of a verse or poetic line, esp. as divided by a caesura

4. **halitosis** (hal′itō′sis)
   (a) castle of a medieval noble
   (b) challah
   (c) foolish or senseless person
   (d) bad breath

5. **hormone** (hôr′mōn)
   (a) large bloodsucking fly that is a serious pest to horses, cattle, etc.

    (b)  small harmless lizard with flattened body and horn-like spines

    (c)  thin, pliable layer of animal or vegetable tissue, serving to line an organ or connect parts

    (d)  compound secreted in endocrine organs and affecting the functions of other organs or tissues

6.  **bourgeois**  (boŏrzhwä′)
    (a)  lady's private sitting room, esp. in the Victorian era
    (b)  member of the middle class
    (c)  bunch of flowers
    (d)  generous advice

7.  **incognito**  (in·kog′nitō′)
    (a)  mixed together
    (b)  related by birth
    (c)  under an assumed name
    (d)  within the jurisdiction of a court

8.  **to rasp**  (rasp)
    (a)  to make a grating sound
    (b)  to cut a thin slice of bacon for frying or boiling
    (c)  to preserve dark red berries of a prickly shrub
    (d)  to make or become rare

9  **immature**  (im′ətoŏr′)
    (a)  actively poisonous or harmful
    (b)  pertaining to a rectangular harpsichord popular in the sixteenth century
    (c)  lusterless and dull in surface
    (d)  not mature

10.  **pacifism**  (pas′əfiz′əm)
    (a)  calm and quiet disposition
    (b)  unusual agreement
    (c)  opposition to violence as a method of settling disputes
    (d)  dark blue coloration of the sky

Correct answers: 1 (c), 2 (c), 3 (a), 4 (d), 5 (d), 6 (b), 7 (c), 8 (a), 9 (d), 10 (c)

Your score: _____
(10 correct: superb; 9–7 correct: good; 6–5 correct: fair)

# Word Roots, Test A

Each of the following ten words stems from one of the three sources shown. Mark the correct answer.

1. pencil
    (a) from Greek *poine*, "fine"
    (b) from Latin *punctiare*, "to prick"
    (c) from Latin *penicillus*, "painter's brush or pencil" (literally, "little tail")

2. knapsack
    (a) from Middle English *nappen*, "to sleep"
    (b) from "*nape* (of the neck)" plus *sack*
    (c) from Low German *knapp*, "bite (of food)"

3. billy—police officer's club
    (a) from Old English *bill*, "sword"
    (b) from Late Latin *bulla*, "bull"
    (c) from the horn of a *billy* goat

4. contraband
    (a) from Latin *contra bonos mores*, "contrary to good manners"
    (b) from Italian *contrabbando*, "against the law"
    (c) from Latin *contractio*, "a drawing together"

5. easel
    (a) from Old French *aise*, "ease"
    (b) from Old English *eastre*, "Easter"
    (c) from Dutch *ezel*, "ass"

6. dray
    (a) from Old English *dreogan*, "to endure"
    (b) from Old English *dragan*, "to draw"
    (c) from Middle Dutch *docke*, "doll"

13

7. canopy
   (a) from French *canard*, "hoax"
   (b) from Old English *canonic*, "one under rule"
   (c) from Greek *konopeion*, "mosquito net"

8. pintle—pin or bolt on which a hinge turns
   (a) from Dutch *pinkje*, "pinkie, or little finger"
   (b) from Latin *pinea*, "pine cone"
   (c) from Old English *pintel*, "penis"

9. chiffon
   (a) from Swiss German *schiffli*, "little ship"
   (b) from *chiffonier* (high chest of drawers)
   (c) from French *chiffe*, "rag"

10. epistle
    (a) from Greek *episteme*, "knowledge"
    (b) from Greek *epistole*, "message"
    (c) from Greek *epitaphion*, "on a tomb"

---

Correct answers: 1 (c), 2 (c), 3 (a), 4 (b), 5 (c), 6 (b), 7 (c), 8 (c), 9 (c), 10 (b)

Your score: _____
(10–9 correct: superb; 8–6 correct: good; 5–4 correct: fair)

14

# From the Land of the Puzzlingly Intricate

by Henry and Renée Kahane

In the relentless succession of dominant cultures that, each at its time, turned into the models of modernism and know-how, Byzantium had its day a thousand years ago. Western Europe was awakening from the breakdown of the Roman Empire and eagerly imported all kinds of innovations from its glamorous Eastern neighbor, often with their names. Byzantium is long gone, but its gifts are still very much alive, with their provenience hidden behind many of our "household" words.

Three examples:

1. *Travail* and *travel*. In the late centuries of the ancient world, the Byzantine punitive system used a tool of torture that consisted of three pieces of timber crudely put together. It was called, therefore, *tripassalon*, a "three-stake." In the early Middle Ages that tool proved useful to the Westerners; it was adopted, and its name, as it often goes with imported things, was translated from Greek into Latin. It became known as *tripalium*. The memory of this instrument of torture remained alive through the centuries, and the most disagreeable things life could offer were called after it. Thus, the French still today call work *travail*, and from them we got the English *travail*, but also our *travel*, which must have been a rather bothersome experience to our ancestors.

2. *Risk*. Egypt was an important province of the Byzantine Empire, but in the seventh century Islam conquered it and established there a military government. The Arabic soldiers were not paid but had to live on the land by taking what they could get. They referred to this system of sustenance with an Arabic word that the Greeks in Egypt heard as *rizikón*, and the Greeks borrowed the word and shifted its use from the soldier's right to requisition to his luck, good or bad, in finding his maintenance, and finally generalized it to "chance

15

and fate." It was the beginning of Western mercenary soldiery. Later, in the twelfth century, with the expanded Mediterranean trade, *rizikón* became a term of maritime law and insurance applied to the dangers of the sea. Through the Italian republics, such as Venice, *risicum* and the shorter *riscum* became international words. Our modern *risk* still preserves these two roots of its past, the military and the nautical, the chance and the danger. *Risk* has become, indeed, a key term of our modern life style.

3. *Diaper*. With ever new fashions to be displayed at Court, the Byzantine textile industry gained international prestige. In the tenth century, a new technique of weaving developed in which two tones of the same color were set against each other, and a fine fabric with two shades of white was called *diaspron*, "twice white." It was exported to the West, where the "jet set" loved it, keeping the Byzantine name as *diasprum*. Through France it reached England, and in English we still know and love that once twice-white damask as *diaper*.

*Dr. Henry Kahane and Dr. Renée Kahane are Professors of Linguistics at the University of Illinois, Urbana-Champaign.*

# Chapter II

## Vocabulary Test No. 4

Which word or phrase is nearest in meaning to each of the following headwords from a press conference held by President Reagan?

1. rebel   (reb'əl)
    (a) accountant (of low rank) connected with the U.S. Treasury
    (b) person who engages in armed resistance against an established government
    (c) abrupt, often blunt, refusal
    (d) one who obstinately defies authority or discipline

2. ethics   (eth'iks)
    (a) group of people of the same race or nationality sharing common and distinctive cultural characteristics
    (b) prescribed or accepted code of usage in matters of ceremony
    (c) underlying sentiments that influence the beliefs of a society
    (d) a system of moral principles

3. totalitarian   (tōtal'itâr'ē·ən)
    (a) pertaining to one-man rule
    (b) pertaining to a car-wrecking business
    (c) pertaining to the highest order of mathematics
    (d) pertaining to a government in which authoritarian political control is concentrated in one party

4. poverty   (pov′ərtē)
   (a) lack of money, goods, or means of support
   (b) alms
   (c) person or group with great energy or potential for success
   (d) jellybean made of almonds or pecans or other nuts

5. veto   (vē′tō)
   (a) act of annoyance
   (b) power vested in a person or branch of government to cancel or postpone another's decisions or enactments
   (c) something that covers like a garment
   (d) son of a veterinarian

6. envy   (en′vē)
   (a) speech or writing in praise of a person or thing
   (b) discontent or jealousy about another's good fortune
   (c) the study of historical linguistic change, esp. as applied to individual words
   (d) discontented boredom

7. to flare   (flâr)
   (a) to develop or erupt suddenly
   (b) to show intense nervous excitement
   (c) to defend or guard at the flank
   (d) to "lay low"

8. discrimination   (diskrim′ənā′shən)
   (a) distinction in favor of or against a person or thing on the basis of prejudice
   (b) resolution
   (c) search for underground water or metal by divining rod
   (d) distillation of ideas

9. munitions   (myo͞onish′ənz)
   (a) incendiary fuses
   (b) transmission of two or more signals or messages simultaneously on the same circuit or channel
   (c) materials used in war, esp. weapons and ammunition
   (d) small-arms fire at close range

10. denigrating (den'əgrāt'ing)
    (a) claiming that white is black, black is white
    (b) attacking (someone's) reputation
    (c) removing chemical ingredients from a test tube
    (d) doubting the quality of life

---

Correct answers: 1 (b), 2 (d), 3 (d), 4 (a), 5 (b), 6 (b), 7 (a), 8 (a), 9 (c), 10 (b)

Your score:_____
(10 correct: superb; 9–7 correct: good; 6–5 correct: fair)

19

# Over There

You're in London and you're told you're a ripping fellow.
Should you put your dukes up?
See how jolly well you know your British English.

| BRITISH ENGLISH | AMERICAN ENGLISH |
|---|---|
| 1. ripping | _____ |
| 2. funfair | _____ |
| 3. rover | _____ |
| 4. bonnet | _____ |
| 5. valve | _____ |
| 6. maize | _____ |
| 7. dustbin | _____ |
| 8. torch | _____ |
| 9. ratable | _____ |
| 10. van | _____ |
| 11. waistcoat | _____ |
| 12. pram | _____ |
| 13. cracker | _____ |
| 14. slavey | _____ |
| 15. ring road | _____ |
| 16. wigging | _____ |
| 17. mercer | _____ |
| 18. underground | _____ |
| 19. solicitor | _____ |
| 20. way out | _____ |

Correct answers: 1. splendid; 2. amusement park; 3. person holding a ticket at a concert for standing room only; 4. automobile hood; 5. vacuum tube; 6. corn; 7. garbage can; 8. flashlight; 9. liable to taxation; 10. railway baggage car; 11. vest; 12. perambulator; 13. biscuit; 14. maid for all work; 15. beltway; 16. scolding; 17. dealer in textiles; 18. subway; 19. lawyer who practices in the lower courts, gives legal advice, and assists barristers; 20. exit (exit sign, as in a theater)

Your score: _____
(20–18 correct: superb; 17–14 correct: good; 13–11 correct: fair)

# Vocabulary Test No. 5

Which word or phrase is nearest in meaning to each of the following headwords from Holocaust literature?

1. holocaust   (hol'əkôst')
   (a) mass execution of religious figures
   (b) devastation, esp. by fire
   (c) imprisonment of persons because of race or religion
   (d) inquisition

2. genocide   (jen'əsīd')
   (a) removal by surgery of genes deemed detrimental to the state
   (b) systematic extermination of a national or racial group
   (c) the coming into being of something, esp. through a process of development
   (d) amputation of the sexual organs

3. ghetto   (get'ō)
   (a) a section of a city inhabited predominantly by a minority group
   (b) business section of any middle-European city
   (c) island in Venice
   (d) small, immature cucumber, used in pickling for religious holidays

4. stereotype   (ster'ē·ətīp')
   (a) political lie
   (b) antibiotic produced by a fungus found in soil and denied universally to inmates of concentration camps in Germany
   (c) hateful headlines
   (d) idea of expression lacking in freshness or originality

5. **Aryan**   (âr′ē·ən)
   (a)   non-Jewish Caucasian (in Nazi doctrine)
   (b)   long-time resident (in Nazi doctrine, before Napoleon's conquest)
   (c)   non-white professor dismissed from tenured position
   (d)   member of the Nazi party

6. **malediction**   (mal′idik′shən)
   (a)   faulty or anomalous structure, esp. in a living body
   (b)   harmful untruths
   (c)   curse
   (d)   preparation of anti-Semitic newspapers

7. **catalepsy**   (kat′′lep′sē)
   (a)   physical condition characterized by suspension of sensation, muscular rigidity, etc.
   (b)   sexual intercourse in a confined area
   (c)   summary of the principles of a religion, usually in the form of questions and answers
   (d)   attack by armored vehicles

8. **pogrom**   (pəgrum′)
   (a)   expropriation of businesses
   (b)   organized massacre, esp. of Jews
   (c)   public humiliation
   (d)   mass stripping of prisoners regardless of gender

9. **progeny**   (proj′ənē)
   (a)   prison squealers or tattletales
   (b)   descendants or offspring collectively
   (c)   forecast of the probable course of government action
   (d)   utterly and shamelessly immoral decision

10. **descent**   (disent′)
   (a)   smell of fire
   (b)   disagreement, esp. on political issues
   (c)   knowledge of just what to do in any situation
   (d)   lineage or ancestry

23

**Correct answers:** 1 (b), 2 (b), 3 (a), 4 (d), 5 (a), 6 (c), 7 (a), 8 (b), 9 (b), 10 (d)

**Your score:** _____
(10 correct: superb; 9–7 correct: good; 6–5 correct: fair)

# There *Is* a Word for It

Example:
a heavy iron block on which metals are hammered into desired shapes: a _____

The answer is "anvil."

1. a first-year cadet in the U.S. Air Force Academy:
   d _____

2. a strong, twilled fabric used esp. for clothing:
   s _____

3. a slender wire nail having a small, deep head:
   b _____

4. a hot, dusty wind blowing from North Africa into southern Europe: s _____

5. a strong-scented, weedy herb having yellow flowers:
   t _____

6. a small, round skullcap worn by Roman Catholic ecclesiastics: z _____

7. a figure of speech combining incongruous or contradictory ideas: o _____

8. in excess of the regular or required number; in the theater, a performer with no speaking lines:
   s _____

9. the vertical groove on the surface of the upper lip:
   p _____

10. a wild, noisy fight: d_____

_____

Correct answers: 1. doolie 2. serge 3. brad 4. sirocco 5. tansy 6. zucchetto 7. oxymoron 8. supernumerary 9. philtrum 10. donnybrook

Your score:_____
(10–9 correct: superb; 8–6 correct: good; 5–4 correct: fair)

# Vocabulary Test No. 6

Which word or phrase is nearest in meaning to each of the following headwords?

1. skepticism (skep'tisiz'əm)
   (a) argument of the Salem "witches" that led to their hanging
   (b) oblique course
   (c) doubt with regard to a religion; the philosophical doctrine that no knowledge is trustworthy
   (d) tenure of a long-time prisoner in a federal cell

2. subjective (səbjek'tiv)
   (a) belonging to the thinking person rather than to the object of thought
   (b) enslaved
   (c) under consideration
   (d) introducing a sentence

3. relativity (rel'ətiv'itē)
   (a) positive data
   (b) connection with others by blood or marriage
   (c) disproportionate weight of a simple argument
   (d) the theory that matter and energy are equivalent and form the basis for nuclear energy and that space and time are not absolute concepts

4. sovereign (sov'rin)
   (a) having supreme rank or power
   (b) given or kept as a reminder (as of a place visited)
   (c) in great pain
   (d) dominated by inclement weather

5. **fallible** (fal'əbəl)
   - (a) liable to err or be mistaken
   - (b) collapsing under the weight of snow
   - (c) vulnerable
   - (d) blooming in autumn

6. **valid** (val'id)
   - (a) soundly founded on fact or evidence
   - (b) unconscious (Freud's term)
   - (c) living in a valley
   - (d) cut off by a valve

7. **hierarchy** (hī'ərär'kē)
   - (a) first line of defense that falls in a philosophic argument
   - (b) rule by mailed fist
   - (c) government by an elite group
   - (d) hymen

8. **dogma** (dôg'mə)
   - (a) maternal faith that no member of the family can do wrong
   - (b) system of principles or tenets, as of a church
   - (c) cynical approach to economic theory
   - (d) star cluster 4.3 light-years from Earth

9. **intrinsic** (intrin'sik)
   - (a) arousing curiosity or interest
   - (b) belonging to a thing by its very nature
   - (c) within or into a vein or the veins
   - (d) at the top or on a high branch of a Christmas tree

10. **corollary** (kôr'əler'ē)
    - (a) dirge (in Scotland and Ireland)
    - (b) public official whose chief function is to investigate any death not clearly resulting from natural causes
    - (c) proposition that is incidentally proved in proving another proposition
    - (d) figure of speech in which two unlike things are explicitly compared

**Correct answers:** 1 (c), 2 (a), 3 (d), 4 (a), 5 (a), 6 (a), 7 (c), 8 (b), 9 (b), 10 (c)

**Your score:** _____
(10 correct: superb; 9–7 correct: good; 6–5 correct: fair)

# Word Roots, Test B

Each of the following ten words stems from one of the three sources shown. Mark the correct answer.

1. cosmic
   - (a) from Hebrew *kasher*, "right"
   - (b) from Greek *kosmos*, "world"
   - (c) from Greek *katholikos*, "universal"

2. eclipse
   - (a) from Greek *ekdyein*, "to strip off (clothing)"
   - (b) from Old English *clyppan*, "to embrace"
   - (c) from Greek *ekleipein*, "to fail to appear"

3. aureole
   - (a) from Latin *aureola*, "golden"
   - (b) from Greek *aura*, "breeze, breath"
   - (c) from Latin *ore rotundo*, "with round mouth"

4. luminary
   - (a) from Medieval Latin *luminaria*, "lamp"
   - (b) from *Luna*, the Roman moon goddess
   - (c) a word coined by Shakespeare meaning (today) "bit player," of unknown derivation

5. iceberg
   - (a) from Greek *isobathes*, "of equal depth"
   - (b) from Dutch *ijsberg*, "ice mountain"
   - (c) from Greek *ichtyhys*, "fish"

6. torrent
   - (a) from Irish *toiridhe*, "highwayman"
   - (b) from Latin *torrens*, "boiling stream"
   - (c) from Latin *torpidus*, "benumbed"

7. **ooze**
   - (a) from the Wizard of *Oz*'s slimy successor
   - (b) from Greek *ozein*, "to smell"
   - (c) from Old English *wase*, "puddle"

8. **reservoir**
   - (a) from Late Latin *reservatorium*, "storehouse"
   - (b) from Latin *resectio*, "a cutting off"
   - (c) from Latin *residuum*, "residue"

9. **boondocks**
   - (a) from Tagalog *bundok*, "mountain"
   - (b) a word coined by a North Carolina Senator (in 1835), of unknown derivation
   - (c) from Dutch *bommen*, "to boom"

10. **canyon**
   - (a) from Spanish *cañón*, "long tube"
   - (b) from Chinese *kaoling*, "mountain"
   - (c) from a comic strip created by Milton Cuniff, of unknown derivation

---

Correct answers: 1 (b), 2 (c), 3 (a), 4 (a), 5 (b), 6 (b), 7 (c), 8 (a), 9 (a), 10 (a)

Your score:_____
(10–9 correct: superb; 8–6 correct: good; 5–4 correct: fair)

# Talking about Mavericks

by Sol Steinmetz

*Gobbledygook*, "pretentious verbiage; bureaucratic jargon; officialese," is one of the more successful coinages of our time, worthy of standing side by side with Lewis Carroll's *jabberwocky*. It was coined by a man whose own name had entered the English language as a synonym for nonconformity. The man was the redoubtable Maury Maverick (1895–1954), the grandson of another formidable figure, Sam Maverick, who had been a Texas cattle owner, a mayor of San Antonio, and a signer of the Texas Declaration of Independence. Sam Maverick refused to brand his cattle, so any unbranded calf came to be called in the 1860s a *maverick*; by 1886, the word was being applied to an unaffiliated or nonconformist politician, and thereafter to any rugged individualist. More surprisingly, Maury Maverick's ancestry included also Judge Charles Lynch, from whose name was derived the verb *lynch*.

With such a background, Maury's future had to be in the law and politics. Like his grandfather, he became mayor of San Antonio (in the 1930s), but before that he served as a congressman, drawing to him a group of insurgent liberal New Dealers in the House of Representatives who were called "mavericks." Maverick was also a prolific writer who, in 1937, published an autobiography, *A Maverick American*, which was praised for its humor and absence of "pomposity and ponderosity." During the Second World War, he served as a government official in various important administrative posts, culminating in his chairmanship of the SWPC, or Smaller War Plants Corporation. In this position, he became the small businessman's lobbyist in Washington, attacking big business and bureaucracy and officialdom in general. It was at this point of his career (April, 1944) that he launched an attack against the pompous, vague, polysyllabic verbiage of Washington bureaucracy. According to his own account, he hit spontaneously, in a flash of inspiration (or genius?), on the word *gobbledygook* to characterize such writing and speech, in imitation of the gobbling of the turkey cock "always gobbledy gobbling and strutting with ludicrous pomposity."

The new word was immediately picked up by the press; editorials praising Maverick's denunciation and applauding the word he had coined appeared in newspapers from coast to coast. *Gobbledygook* was a word whose time had come; but only a dyed-in-the-wool Maverick could invent it and make it a part of the language.

*Mr. Steinmetz is the general editor of* The World Book Dictionary *and coeditor of* The Barnhart Dictionary of New English since 1963 *and* The Second Barnhart Dictionary of New English.

# Chapter III

## Vocabulary Test No. 7

Which word or phrase is nearest in meaning to each of the following headwords from the first best-selling paperback, James Hilton's *Lost Horizon*?

1. conscientious  (kon'shē·en'shəs)
   - (a) benevolent
   - (b) careful and painstaking
   - (c) with appropriate action
   - (d) drafted for military service

2. prig  (prig)
   - (a) rope that is hauled to raise the highest mast on a sailing ship
   - (b) mirror on a bicycle
   - (c) person who affects a particular manner to impress others
   - (d) person who adheres smugly to rigid standards of morality

3. to luxuriate  (lugzhŏŏr'ē·āt')
   - (a) to indulge oneself in luxury
   - (b) to own land at the mouth of the Nile
   - (c) to make light of one's accomplishments
   - (d) to reflect sunlight

4. **beatitude** (bē·at'ətōōd')
   - (a) supreme blessedness or happiness
   - (b) steady thumping by a rabbit's foot
   - (c) means of subsistence
   - (d) cosmetologist's research

5. **jovial** (jō'vē·əl)
   - (a) marked by a hearty, joyous humor
   - (b) hurling thunderbolts (in mythology)
   - (c) suicidal
   - (d) pertaining to REM

6. **avalanche** (av'əlanch')
   - (a) overwhelming suddenness and destructiveness
   - (b) cave-in
   - (c) the study of birdlife in the Congo
   - (d) crest of an ocean wave

7. **theocracy** (thē·ok'rəsē)
   - (a) the walking with a mirage
   - (b) land held in return for military service in early England
   - (c) set of theories
   - (d) government by a deity through organized religion

8. **illusion** (ilōō'zhən)
   - (a) view of a long-time sick person, usually of advanced age
   - (b) something that deceives by producing a false impression
   - (c) hanging, tapering mass of ice formed by the freezing of dripping water
   - (d) wicked or bad dream

9. **equanimity** (ē'kwənim'itē)
   - (a) composure, esp. under tension
   - (b) the four horsemen of the apocalypse
   - (c) pithy, instructive saying
   - (d) all things considered

36

10. **tact**  (takt)
    - (a) temperament
    - (b) keen sense of the right thing to say or do
    - (c) wind direction
    - (d) instrument for measuring or indicating the speed of rotation

---

Correct answers: 1 (b), 2 (d), 3 (a), 4 (a), 5 (a), 6 (a), 7 (d), 8 (b), 9 (a), 10 (b)

Your score: _____
(10 correct: superb; 9–7 correct: good; 6–5 correct: fair)

# As We Weren't Saying

The expressions at the left are euphemisms or unnecessarily complicated terms. Match them with the true meaning or the simpler message at the right.

1. nonretained _____

2. to advance toward adjustments _____

3. terminal living _____

4. inner city _____

5. low-income _____

6. disadvantaged _____

7. encore telecast _____

8. coach (adjective) _____

9. genuine-imitation _____

10. previously owned; pre-owned _____

11. marital aids _____

12. correctional facilities _____

13. grief therapist _____

14. an inoperative statement _____

15. dorsal to _____

16. exacerbate _____

(a) God!

(b) to show you've got the idea

(c) to be ambushed

(d) second-class

(e) behind

(f) fired

(g) sexual-activity gadgets

(h) poor

(i) aggravate

(j) rerun

(k) life saver

(l) bombs falling on schools, hospitals, etc.

(m) atomic bomb

(n) good idea

(o) used

(p) to make budget cuts

(q) to overthrow illegally a foreign government

(r) undertaker

17. to engage the enemy on all sides \_\_\_\_\_

18. incontinent ordnance \_\_\_\_\_

19. nuclear warhead \_\_\_\_\_

20. combat emplacement evacuator \_\_\_\_\_

21. personal-preservation flotation device \_\_\_\_\_

22. to destabilize a government \_\_\_\_\_

23. to ameliorate vectors in the aquatic sector \_\_\_\_\_

24. to demonstrate optimum replicable behavior \_\_\_\_\_

25. prioritized considerment \_\_\_\_\_

26. golly! \_\_\_\_\_

(s) to lay water pipes

(t) prisons

(u) ghetto; slum

(v) fake

(w) shovel

(x) poor; black

(y) dying

(z) a lie

---

Correct answers: 1(f), 2 (p), 3 (y), 4 (u), 5 (h), 6 (x), 7 (j), 8 (d), 9 (v), 10 (o), 11 (g), 12 (t), 13 (r), 14 (z), 15 (e), 16 (i), 17 (c), 18 (l), 19 (m), 20 (w), 21 (k), 22 (q), 23 (s), 24 (b), 25 (n), 26 (a)

Your score:_____
(26–24 correct: superb; 23–19 correct: good; 18–14 correct: fair)

# Vocabulary Test No. 8

Which word or phrase is nearest in meaning to each of the following headwords, which are associated with Chinese history?

1. **extraterritoriality** (ek'strətər'itôr'ē·al'itē)
   - (a) immunity from local jurisdiction
   - (b) land owned abroad by a nation
   - (c) haven for shipwrecked sailors
   - (d) large-scale exploration by a fleet

2. **mandarin** (man'dərin)
   - (a) orange grown exclusively in the Far East until the 1920s
   - (b) high public official in the former Chinese Empire
   - (c) chief architect of the Middle Kingdom
   - (d) a type of land-locked canal invented by the Chinese

3. **concubine** (koñg'kyəbīn')
   - (a) planter of rice
   - (b) woman who cohabits with a man to whom she is not married
   - (c) singsong girl
   - (d) matron of a fancyhouse

4. **pigtail** (pig'tāl')
   - (a) fetish
   - (b) sign that the woman is pregnant
   - (c) delicacy at state banquets
   - (d) braid of hair

5. **coolie** (koo'lē)
   - (a) owner of a fleet of rickshaws
   - (b) iceman

    (c)   number-one boy in a mansion in the French Concession of Shanghai
    (d)   unskilled, cheaply employed laborer

6. **missionary** (mish'əner'ē)
    (a)   process server in Peking
    (b)   person sent to spread religion, esp. abroad
    (c)   chief executioner
    (d)   narrator at a monkey play

7. **warlord** (wôr'lôrd')
    (a)   judge of criminal offenses
    (b)   ship built or armed for combat
    (c)   man in charge of a Chinese village
    (d)   warlike military leader

8. **junk** (juñgk)
    (a)   seagoing ship with a flat bottom
    (b)   opium den
    (c)   opium pipe
    (d)   quay

9. **pagoda** (pəgō'də)
    (a)   towerlike, many-storied temple or sacred building
    (b)   fee for entertainment in big-city department store
    (c)   pickpocket
    (d)   small, usually hard, wartlike growth on the forehead

10. **lotus** (lō'təs)
    (a)   multicolored firecracker
    (b)   land size equal to an acre
    (c)   pedicab driven by a woman
    (d)   aquatic plant with shieldlike leaves and showy, solitary flowers

---

Correct answers: 1 (a), 2 (b), 3 (b), 4 (d), 5 (d), 6 (b), 7 (d), 8 (a), 9 (a), 10 (d)

Your score:_____
(10 correct: superb; 9–7 correct: good; 6–5 correct: fair)

# What Our Presidents Didn't Know

Which President—while he was in office—did not know this expression because it was coined or came into usage during the *next* administration?

Example:
psychedelic: _____

The answer is "Harry S Truman." (He was President from 1945 to 1953; the term "psychedelic" was coined—by Dr. Humphry Osmond—in 1956, during Dwight D. Eisenhower's administration.)

1. Babbitt: _____

2. Academy Awards: _____

3. the White House: _____

4. Borax: _____

5. oceanography: _____

6. Wirephoto: _____

7. chloroform: _____

8. laser: _____

9. recycling: _____

10. cornstarch: _____

Correct answers: **1.** Woodrow Wilson, 1913–21; **2.** Calvin Coolidge, 1923–29; **3.** George Washington, 1789–97; **4.** Millard Fillmore, 1850–53; **5.** Millard Fillmore, 1850–53; **6.** Rutherford B. Hayes, 1877–81; **7.** John Quincy Adams, 1825–29; **8.** Harry S Truman, 1945–53; **9.** Lyndon B. Johnson, 1963–69; **10.** Martin Van Buren, 1837–41

Your score: _____
(10–8 correct: superb; 7–4 correct: good; 3–2 correct: fair)

## Vocabulary Test No. 9

Which word or phrase is nearest in meaning to each of the following headwords, which were used by Franklin Roosevelt in his thirteen years as President?

1. infamy   (in'fəmē)
   (a) exemption from liability to error
   (b) extremely bad reputation as the result of a shameful or criminal act
   (c) secret knowledge or information
   (d) a sense of a national depression

2. contagion   (kəntā'jən)
   (a) inclusion within a volume or area
   (b) infectious ideas
   (c) remark not well-suited for the occasion
   (d) communication of disease by contact

3. rendezvous   (rän'dəvoo')
   (a) interpretation, as of a new piece of legislation
   (b) agreement to meet at a certain time and place
   (c) breakdown of fat
   (d) collision course

4. quarantine   (kwôr'əntēn')
   (a) strict isolation imposed to prevent the spread of disease
   (b) any of three types of elementary particles that are believed to form the basis of all matter
   (c) very small, indivisible quantity of energy
   (d) blockade

5. arsenal   (är'sən'l)
   (a) usurpation
   (b) usury

  (c) supply of weapons
  (d) long-range artillery


6. **to entrench** (entrench′)
  (a) to ask or beg imploringly
  (b) to tear away the outer layer of skin
  (c) to dig trenches for defensive purposes
  (d) to ship (something) to Europe, esp. for military purposes


7. **dynasty** (dī′nəstē)
  (a) belief in reincarnation
  (b) sequence of rulers from the same family or group
  (c) impairment of the ability to read due to a brain defect
  (d) hungry and land-grabbing nation


8. **royalist** (roi′əlist)
  (a) supporter of a king
  (b) ambassador making his first call on the host monarch
  (c) recessed alcove concealing a king's w.c.
  (d) writer who is able to live on income from the sale of his books


9. **alien** (āl′yən)
  (a) ailing immigrant
  (b) psychiatrist, esp. one who specializes in legal matters
  (c) foreigner or stranger
  (d) food donated to starving adults


10. **anonymous** (ənon′əməs)
  (a) without any name acknowledged as that of author
  (b) causing malaria in American troops in the South Pacific
  (c) forthcoming
  (d) without social norms, as in the case of uprooted people

Correct answers: 1 (b), 2 (d), 3 (b), 4 (a), 5 (c), 6 (c), 7 (b), 8 (a), 9 (c), 10 (a)

Your score:_____
(10 correct: superb; 9–7 correct: good; 6–5 correct: fair)

# Word Roots, Test C

Each of the following ten words stems from one of the three sources shown. Mark the correct answer.

1. **soldier**
   (a) from Latin *solidus*, "pay"
   (b) from Latin *solea*, "flatfish"
   (c) from the Greek town *Soloi*, known for its corrupt citizenry

2. **guerrilla**
   (a) the name of a nation in Chad
   (b) from Middle English *grofling*, "with the face downward"
   (c) diminutive of Spanish *guerra*, "war"

3. **battle**
   (a) from Middle French *battre*, "to beat"
   (b) from Latin *battualia*, "gladiatorial exercises"
   (c) from "(who is) *better*"

4. **fort**
   (a) from Latin *fortis*, "strong"
   (b) from Charles *Fort*, the pseudoscientist who claimed that flying saucers clashed over Burlington, Vt., in the early 1900s
   (c) from *Hamlet*'s *Fortinbras*, who spoke of "carnal, bloody, and unnatural acts...casual slaughters..."

5. **petard**— explosive device formerly used to blow in doors or make breaches in walls
   (a) from Latin *petitionis*, "to seek"
   (b) from Latin *petulantia*, "impudence"
   (c) from Middle French *peter*, "to break wind"

6. shambles
   (a) from Hindi *champna*, "to press"
   (b) from Henry VIII's court jester, *Shambles*
   (c) from Middle English *shamel*, "bench"

7. to conquer
   (a) from Latin *conquirere*, "to search for, to procure"
   (b) from Latin *concordia*, "agreement"
   (c) from *Concordia*, the Roman goddess of peace

8. sabotage
   (a) from Hebrew *shabath*, "to rest"
   (b) from French *sabre*, "saber"
   (c) from French *sabot*, "wooden shoe"

9. conscript
   (a) from Latin *conscribere*, "to enroll"
   (b) from Chinese *k'o-t'o*, "to bump the head (on the floor)"
   (c) from Late Latin *comes stabuli*, "count of the stable"

10. to beleaguer
    (a) from Old English *bealcian*, "belch"
    (b) from Dutch *belegeren*, "to camp around"
    (c) from Old English *geleafa*, "belief"

---

Correct answers: 1 (a), 2 (c), 3 (b), 4 (a), 5 (c), 6 (c), 7 (a), 8 (c), 9 (a), 10 (b)

Your score: _____
(10–9 correct: superb; 8–6 correct: good; 5–4 correct: fair)

# A Mountain out of a Molehill

## by Isaac Asimov

To the Greeks, *chaos* was primeval matter in total disorder. *Cosmos*, on the other hand, was that same matter in some appearance of order.

The creation of the universe, then, was not the creation of matter; that already existed. It was the creation of *order*.

Anything that imposes disorder on matter originally in order is *chaotic*. On the other hand, anything that imposes order on matter originally in disorder is *cosmetic*.

And now we know what it is that a woman does when she uses *cosmetics* to *make up* her face.

*At this writing, Dr. Asimov has published 232 books on—everything.*

# Chapter IV

## Vocabulary Test No. 10

Which word or phrase is nearest in meaning to each of the following headwords, which are associated with Marshall McLuhan (*The Medium is the Massage*)?

1. media (mē′dē·ə)
   - (a) piece of music combining tunes or passages from various sources
   - (b) ordinary or average situation
   - (c) helicopter for evacuating the wounded from a battlefield
   - (d) means of communication that reach or influence very large numbers of people

2. osmosis (ozmō′sis)
   - (a) passage of fluid through a membrane, so as to equalize the concentration on both sides
   - (b) theme of the sole fairy tale in the Five Books of Moses
   - (c) moderate or small quantity
   - (d) sphere or globe

3. remedial (rimē′dē·əl)
   - (a) medical
   - (b) subordinate
   - (c) arbitrating
   - (d) affording relief

51

4. to pervade (pərvād′)
   (a) to read or examine, esp. with care
   (b) to spread through every part
   (c) to have a fit (as of peevishness)
   (d) to explode a device formerly used to blow in a door or gate

5. environment (envī′rənmənt)
   (a) suburban community once considered exurbia
   (b) the aggregate of surrounding conditions
   (c) place offering luxurious and unrestrained pleasure
   (d) field made poisonous by extraction of indigenous fauna

6. commodity (kəmod′itē)
   (a) produced goods owned by everyone in the community
   (b) the ordinary or common people
   (c) something of use or value
   (d) (formerly) a closed cabinet or chair containing a chamber pot

7. sage (sāj)
   (a) expedition for hunting, esp. in eastern Africa
   (b) any living being
   (c) narrative of heroic exploits
   (d) profoundly wise person

8. sublime (səblīm′)
   (a) daydreaming
   (b) feeling under the weather
   (c) elevated or lofty, as thought
   (d) redirected, as an impulse to more socially constructive ends

9. apposition (ap′əzish′ən)
   (a) pertinence
   (b) appointment
   (c) proportion
   (d) act of placing side by side

10. **interface**  (in′tərfās′)
    (a) surface regarded as the common boundary of two things
    (b) distance from nose to nose in social interaction
    (c) Roman mask
    (d) successful disguise

---

**Correct answers:** 1 (d), 2 (a), 3 (d), 4 (b), 5 (b), 6 (c), 7 (d), 8 (c), 9 (d), 10 (a)

**Your score:** _____
(10–9 correct: superb; 8–6 correct: good; 5–4 correct: fair)

# Eponyms

The items at the left refer to proper names; the items at the right define words or phrases that are derived from these proper names. Match them.

Example:
a hotel in Manhattan _____     a salad of celery, diced apples, nuts, and mayonnaise

The answer is "Waldorf salad" (Waldorf-Astoria Hotel).

1. a town in Ireland _____

2. a British general _____

3. a Spanish town _____

4. an atoll in the Marshall Islands _____

5. the Hospital of St. Mary of Bethlehem, in London _____

6. a fishmarket in London _____

7. a city in Russia _____

8. islands north of Scotland _____

9. a Greek port _____

10. an Athenian statesman _____

(a) a scene of wild uproar and confusion

(b) oppressively severe

(c) a hollow projectile containing bullets designed to explode before reaching the target

(d) coarsely or vulgarly abusive language

(e) a fur of young lambs, with lustrous, closely curled wool

(f) a cudgel, traditionally of blackthorn or oak

(g) a very brief two-piece bathing suit for women

(h) a small seedless raisin

(i) one of a breed of hardy shaggy ponies with long manes and tails

(j) a pale, dry sherry

Correct answers: 1 (f) shillelagh (Shillelagh), 2 (c) shrapnel (H. Shrapnel, 1761–1842), 3 (j) amontillado (Montilla), 4 (g) bikini (Bikini), 5 (a) bedlam (short for Bethlehem), 6 (d) billingsgate (Billingsgate), 7 (e) astrakhan (Astrakhan), 8 (i) Shetland pony (the Shetlands), 9 (h) currant (Corinth), 10 (b) Draconian (Draco, seventh century B.C., noted for his severe laws)

Your score: _____
(10–9 correct: superb; 8–6 correct: good; 5–4 correct: fair)

# Vocabulary Test No. 11

Which word or phrase is nearest in meaning to each of the following headwords from George Orwell's *Nineteen Eighty-Four*?

1. mystical    (mis'tikəl)
   (a) suited for voodoo rites
   (b) seeing ghostly images emerging from a fog-shrouded moor
   (c) of occult character or power
   (d) magical (like Merlin)

2. ferocity    (fəros'itē)
   (a) savage fierceness
   (b) unexpected blow on the back
   (c) alloy used in the making of jet engines
   (d) cold wind that sweeps across Europe from the east

3. entrails    (en'trālz)
   (a) smoke that a jet airplane emits
   (b) the best known omen of an impending earthquake
   (c) three-way road by which condemned persons must at some time stand
   (d) internal parts of an animal, esp. the intestine

4. statutory    (stach'ōotōr'ē)
   (a) pertaining to the monuments to leaders of state
   (b) legally punishable, as an offense
   (c) legal but controversial
   (d) higher than any person or animal

5. timorous    (tim'ərəs)
   (a) overly or fearfully timid
   (b) too great to express in words
   (c) of slight coloration
   (d) used as fodder

56

6. **labyrinth** (lab'ərinth)
   - (a) inner folds of skin bordering the vulva
   - (b) change, esp. in chemistry
   - (c) system of many twisting passages or paths out of which it is hard to find one's way
   - (d) circular tub

7. **sedition** (sidish'ən)
   - (a) incitement of public disorder or rebellion against a government
   - (b) right of the bride to cancel the marriage after a suitable length of honeymoon
   - (c) general outpouring of officialdom against colonialists
   - (d) lead editorial in a revolutionary tract

8. **to abase** (əbās')
   - (a) to force (someone) to share a flat
   - (b) to humble or degrade (used usually reflexively)
   - (c) to announce the mobilization of militia
   - (d) to go to the rear

9. **furtive** (fûr'tiv)
   - (a) at the far side of the Moon
   - (b) punished by electricity (in experiments)
   - (c) taken, done, used, etc., by stealth
   - (d) unrestrained or violent

10. **to indoctrinate** (indok'trənāt')
   - (a) to avoid exertion
   - (b) to insist on rote learning
   - (c) to consider individually
   - (d) to instruct in a principle or ideology

---

Correct answers: 1 (c), 2 (a), 3 (d), 4 (b), 5 (a), 6 (c), 7 (a), 8 (b), 9 (c), 10 (d)

Your score: _____
(10–9 correct: superb; 8–6 correct: good; 5–4 correct: fair)

# Fill In the Blanks

Example:
discreet and prudent:

__ __ __ __ u m s __ __ __ __

The answer is "circumspect."

1. any of a group of mammals, the female of which has a pouch for carrying her young:
   __ a r __ __ __ i a l

2. a prayer consisting of a series of invocations with responses: __ __ t a n y

3. addicted to alcoholic drinking: __ __ __ __ l o u s

4. having many curves, bends, or turns:
   __ __ __ __ o u s

5. a minor defect or malfunction in a machine or plan (slang): __ l i t __ __

6. a person or thing that arouses wonder or astonishment: m a __ __ e __

7. a person who is fond of good eating, usually indiscriminately and often to excess:
   __ __ u r __ a n __

8. a low, contemptible scoundrel:
   b __ a __ __ __ __ a r d

9. a newcomer to an unsettled region of the western U.S., unused to hardships; a raw, inexperienced person:
   t e __ __ e __ __ o __ t

10. a sensory experience of something that does not exist outside the mind: __ __ l __ u __ i n a __ i __ __

**Correct answers: 1. marsupial 2. litany 3. bibulous 4. sinuous 5. glitch 6. marvel 7. gourmand 8. blackguard 9. tenderfoot 10. hallucination**

**Your score:** _____
(10–9 correct: superb; 8–6 correct: good; 5–4 correct: fair)

# Vocabulary Test No. 12

Which word or phrase is nearest in meaning to each of the following headwords, which are all "confusibles" (words that sometimes play tricks on the memory)?

1. **to infer** (infûr′)
   - (a) to conclude, or to suppose
   - (b) to inspire with a foolish or unreasoning passion
   - (c) to overrun in a troublesome manner, as vermin
   - (d) to flower and bloom

2. **to imply** (implī′)
   - (a) to insist
   - (b) to make steady inroads
   - (c) to stamp out
   - (d) to indicate, or to hint

3. **notorious** (nōtōr′ē·əs)
   - (a) celebrated
   - (b) widely but unfavorably known
   - (c) having star quality (as a television personality)
   - (d) making diary entries

4. **cavalier** (kav′ə lēr′)
   - (a) one who raises irritating and trivial objections
   - (b) servant who places on the table the roe of sturgeon
   - (c) person having the manner of a courtier
   - (d) the principle that the buyer should beware of the product bought

5. **to ensure** (enshŏŏr′)
   - (a) to secure or guarantee
   - (b) to prohibit by an injunction
   - (c) to move to rapture
   - (d) to exalt or revere

6. **ingenuous** (injen′yoo·əs)
    (a) clever by half
    (b) having seized the moment
    (c) fanciful (said of a teenage girl)
    (d) free from deceit or disguise

7. **ingenious** (injēn′yəs)
    (a) having committed a breach or infraction
    (b) cleverly inventive or resourceful
    (c) clad in tight pants
    (d) in need of confinement to a hospital, prison, etc.

8. **meretricious** (mer′itrish′əs)
    (a) honorable
    (b) having little or no money
    (c) covered by a G-string (in burlesque routine)
    (d) vulgarly attractive

9. **jealous** (jel′əs)
    (a) fatuous or foolish
    (b) troubled by suspicions of rivalry or unfaithfulness
    (c) juvenile or immature
    (d) given to jesting

10. **anxious** (aṅgk′shəs)
    (a) immobilized
    (b) eager or desirous
    (c) very helpful
    (d) moving up and down or to and fro with short, quick
        jerks

---

Correct answers: 1 (a), 2 (d), 3 (b), 4 (c), 5 (a), 6 (d), 7 (b),
8 (d), 9 (b), 10 (b)

Your score:_____
(10–9 correct: superb; 8–6 correct: good; 5–4 correct: fair)

# Word Roots, Test D

Each of the following ten words stems from one of the three sources shown. Mark the correct answer.

1. author
    (a) from Latin *auctor*, "originator"
    (b) from Greek *autarchia*, "self-rule"
    (c) from Italian *artigiano*, "skilled craftsman"

2. umpire
    (a) from French *piquant*, "pricking"
    (b) from Latin *imperiosus*, "dictatorial, overbearing"
    (c) from Old French *nomper*, "peerless"

3. coolie
    (a) from Cantonese *kam kwat*, "golden orange"
    (b) coined by President *Coolidge*, for a White House aide
    (c) from Hindi *kuli*, "day laborer"

4. barber
    (a) from Latin *barba*, "beard"
    (b) from Gael *bard*, "poet"
    (c) from Greek *barbaros*, "foreign"

5. mountebank
    (a) from Spanish *monte*, "mountain"
    (b) from French *monsieur*, "my lord"
    (c) from Italian *montimbanco*, "one who mounts a bench"

6. attorney
    (a) from Anglo-French *attourne*, "turned"
    (b) from Latin *attingere*, "to touch upon"
    (c) from Latin *attritus*, "rubbed away"

7. **scullion**
   (a) from Middle English *sculle*, "scull"
   (b) from Late Latin *excaldare*, "to wash in hot water"
   (c) from Middle French *escouvillon*, "swab"

8. **grenade**
   (a) from the *Grenadines*, a chain of islands in the West Indies
   (b) from Old English *grennian*, "to show the teeth"
   (c) from French *grenade*, "pomegranate"

9. **grocer**
   (a) from Vulgar Latin *crupta*, "crypt"
   (b) from Old French *grossier*, "wholesale dealer"
   (c) from Old French *groseille*, "gooseberry"

10. **tutelage**
    (a) from Latin *tutor*, "guardian"
    (b) from Latin *tutela*, "protection"
    (c) from Latin *totus*, "whole"

---

Correct answers: 1 (a), 2 (c), 3 (c), 4 (a), 5 (c), 6 (a), 7 (c), 8 (c), 9 (b), 10 (b)

Your score: _____
(10–9 correct: superb; 8–6 correct: good; 5–4 correct: fair)

# Double Jeopardy

### by François Gautier

What do these expressions have in common—"a diagonal angle," "an epileptic seizure," "a bunch of grapes," "purple ink," "Greenwich Village"?

They are pleonastic (etymologically speaking):

In Greek, *dia-* means "through, across" and *gonia* means "angle." A "diagonal angle" would be a type of "angle angle" (and "diagonally across" might mean something like "cross-angle-wise across").

The Greek word *epilepsis* means "seizure." An "epileptic seizure" would be a "seizure seizure."

In Anglo-French and Middle French, *grape* or *grappe* meant a "bunch of grapes." But saying "a bunch of grapes" would mean a "bunch of a bunch of grapes."

The Greek word *enkauston* (which became our "ink") meant "purple ink." Our " purple ink" would be "purple purple ink."

The suffix *-wich* in "Greenwich" comes from the Latin word *vicus*, "village." "Greenwich Village" would be the "Green Village Village."

*Mr. Gautier is a trilingual editor and lexicographer who lives in New York City.*

# Chapter V

## Vocabulary Test No. 13

Which word or phrase is nearest in meaning to each of the following headwords associated with the synergistic literature of R. Buckminster Fuller?

1. evolution (ev'əloo'shən)
   (a) invention of the wheel
   (b) the doctrine that humans arrived on Earth from another planet
   (c) any process of formation or growth
   (d) viaduct that carried water from surrounding hills into Rome

2. process (pros'es)
   (a) making nothing out of something, esp. in business
   (b) making something out of nothing, esp. in cultural affairs
   (c) systematic series of actions directed to some end
   (d) the concept that the artist is a distant early-warning figure alerting the populace to forthcoming environmental changes

3. ecology (ikol'əjē)
   (a) branch of biology dealing with the relations between organisms and their environment
   (b) the ruin of the human environment, esp. through the use of pollutants

   (c)  postgraduate work in an Ivy League university
   (d)  the study of rocks and minerals

4.  **geodesic**  (jē'ədes'ik)
   (a)  the study of the architectural writings of R. Buck-minster Fuller
   (b)  half of a perfectly cut egg shell
   (c)  atrium where the Caesars would walk alone
   (d)  shortest line lying on a curved surface and connecting two given points

5.  **visionary**  (vizh'əner'ē)
   (a)  with telescopic eyesight
   (b)  having a reputation for being more often right than wrong
   (c)  given to unreal or impractical ideas
   (d)  miragelike

6.  **metabolism**  (mətab'əliz'əm)
   (a)  smallest organ in the human body
   (b)  process by which protoplasm is produced, maintained, and destroyed, and by means of which energy is made available
   (c)  normal heartbeat
   (d)  the manner in which one is in synchrony with nature

7.  **entropy**  (en'trəpē)
   (a)  flight path of early U.S. rockets
   (b)  fluctuating value of gold on the world market
   (c)  invisible molecules that support steel structures
   (d)  measure of the amount of energy unavailable for work during a natural process

8.  **fate**  (fāt)
   (a)  ultimate power by which the order of things is prescribed
   (b)  decisive event in war
   (c)  the process of decision-making
   (d)  proof that grass is the journeywork of the stars

9. **extinct**   (ikstiñgkt′)
   (a) denoting any group of birds of which there are less than seven known members
   (b) put out (as a fire)
   (c) folklore-related
   (d) not existing now

10. **ideology**   (ī′dē·ol′əjē)
   (a) the best ideas of any community
   (b) the body of doctrines or beliefs that guides a particular individual, class, or culture
   (c) the process of forming ideas or images
   (d) formation of everything by a shaman

---

Correct answers: 1 (c), 2 (c), 3 (a), 4 (d), 5 (c), 6 (b), 7 (d), 8 (a), 9 (d), 10 (b)

Your score:_____
(10–9 correct: superb; 8–6 correct: good; 5–4 correct: fair)

# Scramblings

Each phrase defines the word that follows it in scrambled form. Can you put the eggs back together again?

Example:
an example serving as a model: amgdiarp _____

The answer is "paradigm."

1. places diametrically opposite to each other on the globe: niasedtop _____

2. peevishly quarrelsome; refractory or unruly: cfsoruiat _____

3. actively poisonous or harmful; intensely bitter or spiteful: tneluriv _____

4. secretary: nssmaaieun _____

5. of marriage or the relation of husband and wife: jcloaung _____

6. without sensation or feeling: seeittnnin _____

7. to clear from a charge of guilt or fault: lxetpaceu _____

8. a strong iron grating at the main entrance of a castle that can be let down to prevent passage: tslpliucor _____

9. a method of closing debate and causing an immediate vote to be taken: lreucto _____

10. something wanted or needed: mutaerddsie _____

_____

Correct answers: 1. antipodes 2. fractious 3. virulent 4. amanuensis 5. conjugal 6. insentient 7. exculpate 8. portcullis 9. cloture 10. desideratum

Your score: _____
(10–9 correct: superb; 8–6 correct: good; 5–4 correct: fair)

# Vocabulary Test No. 14

Which word or phrase is nearest in meaning to each of the following headwords from Lord Macaulay's *Horatius at the Bridge*?

1. **diadem** (dī'ədem')
   - (a) mark of distinction
   - (b) crown or cloth headband worn as a symbol of power
   - (c) fiendish plot
   - (d) oval-shaped ruby

2. **sentinel** (sen't'n'l)
   - (a) messenger, usually bearing bad news
   - (b) perception by the senses
   - (c) one who is given to excessive moralizing
   - (d) sentry

3. **vassal** (vas'əl)
   - (a) person owing homage to a superior
   - (b) student at a convent
   - (c) land of very great size owned by a fiefdom rather than by an individual
   - (d) dagger

4. **to gild** (gild)
   - (a) to learn a trade
   - (b) to slay (a gladiator)
   - (c) to give a pleasing or specious aspect (to something)
   - (d) to sound the alarm for a Roman armed force

5. **hind** (hīnd)
   - (a) in eastern Europe
   - (b) hindering
   - (c) situated in the rear or back, esp. of an animal
   - (d) hardly noticeable

6. to augur (ô′gər)
   (a) to predict, as from omens
   (b) to train a watchdog
   (c) _to throw a javelin
   (d) to drill

7. sullen (sul′ən)
   (a) two-wheeled (as a one-horse carriage for a bowman)
   (b) oppressively hot and humid
   (c) defiled
   (d) showing resentment in a gloomy and silent way

8. tawny (tô′nē)
   (a) showy and cheap
   (b) round (like a marble)
   (c) of a dark yellowish color
   (d) tightly drawn, as a rope

9. turret (tûr′it)
   (a) cavalry droppings
   (b) small tower forming part of a larger structure, as of a castle
   (c) East Indian plant imported by the Caesars
   (d) shameful wickedness or depravity

10. crag (krag)
    (a) cramp in the leg during sleep
    (b) steep, rugged rock
    (c) old woman
    (d) rejuvenated cloth

_____

Correct answers: 1 (b), 2 (d), 3 (a), 4 (c), 5 (c), 6 (a), 7 (d), 8 (c), 9 (b), 10 (b)

Your score:_____
(10–9 correct: superb; 8–6 correct: good; 5–4 correct: fair)

# There *Is* a Word for It

Example:
a small tea cake, variously frosted and decorated:

p_____ f_____

The answer is "petit four."

1. scamp, scoundrel, or rascal:
   s_____

2. broken pottery fragment, esp. one of archaeological value:
   p_____

3. a religious meeting held by some churches on New Year's Eve and terminating after midnight:
   w_____ n_____

4. tending to produce conformity by violent or arbitrary means: p_____

5. passing the bounds of what is usual or proper:
   o_____

6. a framework supporting a float extended from the side of a boat for adding stability: o_____

7. a mounted attendant riding before or beside a carriage:
   o_____

8. a person who is morally or sexually unrestrained:
   l_____

9. a person who advocates liberty, esp. with regard to thought or conduct; a person who maintains the doctrine of free will: l _____

10. half-burnt tobacco in the bottom of a pipe after smoking: d _____

_____

Correct answers: 1. scalawag 2. potsherd 3. watch night 4. procrustean 5. outré 6. outrigger 7. outrider 8. libertine 9. libertarian 10. dottle

Your score:_____
(10–9 correct: superb; 8–6 correct: good; 5–4 correct: fair)

# Vocabulary Test No. 15

Which word or phrase is nearest in meaning to each of the
following headwords?

1. **etiology** (ē'tē·ol'əjē)
   (a) happenstance
   (b) the study of the causes of diseases
   (c) implosion
   (d) explosion

2. **fortuitous** (fôrtōō'itəs)
   (a) happening or produced by chance
   (b) visceral
   (c) adding to a monument
   (d) causing physical pain to others (esp. to increase one's
       sexual gratification)

3. **éclat** (āklä')
   (a) French dairy farm
   (b) potency
   (c) dessert favored by Napoleon
   (d) brilliance of success

4. **impetuous** (impech'ōō·əs)
   (a) having an effect or impact
   (b) characterized by rash action
   (c) mischievous
   (d) unseemingly intrusive or rude

5. **flaccid** (flak'sid)
   (a) soft and limp
   (b) not pertinent
   (c) fruitful
   (d) favorable for self-advancement

6. **puissance**   (pyō͞o′isəns)
   (a) power, might, or force
   (b) part of a whole
   (c) cattiness
   (d) fatality

7. **prolific**   (prōlif′ik)
   (a) profligate
   (b) prodigious
   (c) producing abundantly
   (d) extraordinary in size or amount

8. **waspish**   (wos′pi̱sh)
   (a) of the queen bee
   (b) quick to be angry or resentful
   (c) open to question or dispute
   (d) caustic

9. **to fulminate**   (ful′mənāt′)
   (a) to explode with a loud noise
   (b) to be satiated
   (c) to disgust
   (d) to be furious

10. **paroxysm**   (par′əksiz′əm)
    (a) peculiarity of behavior or personality
    (b) revolt
    (c) obnoxiousness
    (d) sudden outburst, as of emotion

---

Correct answers: 1 (b), 2 (a), 3 (d), 4 (b), 5 (a), 6 (a), 7 (c), 8 (b), 9 (a), 10 (d)

Your score: _____
(10–9 correct: superb; 8–6 correct: good; 5–4 correct: fair)

# Word Roots, Test E

Each of the following ten words stems from one of the three sources shown. Mark the correct answer.

1. capital
   (a) from Latin *caput*, "head"
   (b) from Latin *captivatus*, "taken prisoner"
   (c) from Latin *captionis*, "seizure"

2. chateau
   (a) from *Charon*, the boatman who ferried souls across the river Styx to Hades
   (b) from la Grande *Chartreuse*, French Carthusian monastery
   (c) from Latin *castellum*, "fort"

3. cabriolet
   (a) euphemism for second class, of unknown derivation
   (b) from Dutch *kabuis*, "cook's cabin"
   (c) from French *cabriole*, "goat's leap"

4. caboose
   (a) from Dutch *kabuis*, "cook's cabin"
   (b) from Arabic *ka'abah*, "square building"
   (c) gandydaucer slang for *cabin*

5. balcony
   (a) from Old French *balu*, "evil"
   (b) from Old English *balca*, "ridge"
   (c) from Italian *balco*, "scaffold"

6. harbor
   (a) from Arabic *harim*, "forbidden (place)"
   (b) from Old English *herebeorg*, "army quarters"
   (c) from Old French *harneis*, "armor"

76

7. **emporium**
   (a) from *Emporia*, a city in Kansas
   (b) from German *empor*, "upward"
   (c) from Greek *emporos*, "merchant"

8. **promenade**
   (a) from Latin *promiscuus*, "mixed up"
   (b) from Late Latin *prominare*, "to drive (beasts)"
   (c) from Medieval Latin *prolifer*, "bearing offspring"

9. **gargoyle**
   (a) from Middle English *gauren*, "to stare"
   (b) from *Gargantua*, the voracious giant in the satire of the same name by Rabelais
   (c) from Middle French *gargouille*, "throat"

10. **dike**
    (a) from Old English *dic*, "ditch"
    (b) from Latin *dignitas*, "worthiness"
    (c) from Greek *dichroos*, "of two colors"

---

Correct answers: 1 (a), 2 (c), 3 (c), 4 (a), 5 (c), 6 (b), 7 (c), 8 (b), 9 (c), 10 (a)

Your score:_____
(10–9 correct: superb; 8–6 correct: good; 5–4 correct: fair)

# If the Truth Be Told

## by Richard W. Bailey

Some writers on language presume that *etymology* is the study not just of the origins of words but also of their "true" meanings, as if *change* were synonymous with *decay* instead of derived, as it in fact is, from "transaction in the marketplace of one thing of value for another."

Conventional etymologies most often concern word borrowings, how some foreign language provides the source for the word stock of the receptor language. Sometimes more interesting than those borrowings, however, are the etymologies that trace the rise and fall through history within a language of the social context of words or the narrowing or spread of denotation. In English, words both rise and fall, but they most often fall: *varlet* descends from "young nobleman" to "scoundrel" (while its cognate *valet* retains some of the respectability of the original sense), and *hussy* declines from "thrifty woman" to "jade" (*jade*, meanwhile, moving from "an unruly horse" to human unruliness). Narrow definitions tend to broaden: *unique*, for instance, from "one-of-a-kind" to "unusual," and *soon* from "immediately" to "after a while." Sometimes breadth of application yields to a more special sense: *deer*, at an earlier time in English, might apply generically to a variety of creatures (a camel was called a "big deer" in an Englishing of the parable from Luke in which we are invited to imagine the difficulty of passing that large beast through the eye of a needle). Later on in English, of course, *deer* was narrowed in its application to the creatures whose male adults are called *stag* or *buck* (and those words, too, acquired human application in *stag party* and *young buck*).

Etymology, then, should address itself to issues beyond the filiation of one language and another. (We English-users are now great exporters of words that purists in other languages complain about: the French Academy denouncing Franglais—*français*, "French," plus *anglais*, "English", like *le weekend*—and the learned in East Africa parodying *Swa-*

*lengleza,* the off-spring of English and ki-Swahili.) Thus, beyond the import-export trade in words and phrases, etymologizers should be equally intrigued by change within a language. Some of these changes are slow-moving; in others, the competing senses of a word may coexist until one gradually replaces the other (as now seems to be happening with the movement of *disinterested* from "impartial" to "bored"); in still others, the pattern of growth and spread is explosively rapid (for instance, *-gate* from *Watergate* to a generalized suffix meaning political scandal and attaching itself to nouns in *Koreagate* (for the shenanigans associated with Tongsun Park), *Lancegate* (for the lending practices of Bert Lance), or *Donovangate* (for the alleged gangland connections of the Secretary of Labor).

The etymology of *etymology* arrives in English from Greek through Latin: "the study of the origin of words" (*etymon* plus *logia*). And *etymos* and its related form *eteos* mean "true." In the English Renaissance, when the revival of classical learning brought *etymology* into our language, the study of words was a way of finding out truth. If we cannot always tell the truth about our words (because we are obliged to record "origin unknown"), our words can tell truths about ourselves and about the history of our culture.

*Dr. Bailey is Professor of English at the University of Michigan.*

# Chapter VI

## Vocabulary Test No. 16

Which word or phrase is nearest in meaning to each of the following headwords from Martin Cruz Smith's thriller, *Gorky Park*?

1. **homicide** (hom′isīd′)
   - (a) murder of a czar by a member of his family
   - (b) murder by chance
   - (c) the killing of one human being by another
   - (d) chief investigator of a police murder unit

2. **greatcoat** (grāt′kōt′)
   - (a) woolen underwear in the Soviet Union
   - (b) tool used in fixing flat tires
   - (c) heavy overcoat
   - (d) hood of a pre–World War Two automobile

3. **dossier** (dos′ē·ā′)
   - (a) list of negative factors about an individual, esp. royalty
   - (b) group of documents on the same subject
   - (c) dental work, esp. construction of a bridge
   - (d) knife used in anatomy to pierce the eyeball

4. **narcolepsy** (när′kəlep′sē)
   - (a) form of brainwashing, developed during the Korean War by the Chinese
   - (b) serum used to drug skin-ravaged patients

81

(c) superpowerful magnifying glass
(d) uncontrollable need for sleep

5. to embezzle   (embez′əl)
   (a) to remove the mouthpiece (of a wind instrument)
   (b) to appropriate fraudulently
   (c) to dazzle
   (d) to prepare oneself for battle

6. grimace   (grim′əs)
   (a) facial expression that indicates disapproval, pain, etc.
   (b) stern and unyielding attitude
   (c) dirt or foul matter, esp. lying upon or embedded in a surface
   (d) fluid jetted into an attacker's face

7. proviso   (prəvī′zō)
   (a) clause in a statute or contract
   (b) slum of a medium-sized city
   (c) proponent of capital punishment
   (d) document allowing free rent for a specified period

8. prudent   (prood′ənt)
   (a) cautious in practical affairs
   (b) small in stature or figure (usually a woman)
   (c) pertaining to the place of origin, as of a work of art
   (d) excessively proper or modest in speech or dress

9. to reverberate   (rivûr′bərāt′)
   (a) to come crashing down
   (b) to repeat at least thrice
   (c) to use a sentence in which the word of action is the most important word
   (d) to be reflected many times, as sound waves

10. to malinger   (məling′gər)
    (a) to carry in a pouch (Australian)
    (b) to be prone to seasickness
    (c) to pretend illness in order to avoid duty or work
    (d) to have an unpleasant odor

Correct answers: 1 (c), 2 (c), 3 (b), 4 (d), 5 (b), 6 (a), 7 (a), 8 (a), 9 (d), 10 (c)

Your score: _____
(10–9 correct: superb; 8–6 correct: good; 5–4 correct: fair)

## Coiners of the Realm

Match these twenty-five words with their creators.

1. ecology _____
2. superman _____
3. deism _____
4. anticlimax _____
5. complex _____
6. avion _____
7. neon _____
8. nihilism _____
9. krypton _____
10. genetics _____
11. deleterious _____
12. microbe _____
13. X-rays _____
14. hypnotism _____
15. Zionism _____
16. neoplasm _____
17. enzyme _____
18. kaleidoscope _____
19. gas _____
20. antibiotics _____
21. parachute _____
22. gastritis _____
23. chromosome _____
24. normalcy _____
25. Achilles' tendon _____

(a) was coined by the English biologist William Bateson (1861–1926).

(b) was coined in 1878 by the German physiologist Wilhelm Kuhne (1837–1900), from the Greek for "leavened."

(c) was coined by the German philosopher F. H. Jacobi (1743–1819), from the Latin for "nothing."

(d) was introduced by the English physician Sir Thomas Browne (1605–82).

(e) was the name coined in 1896 by their discoverer, the German scientist Konrad von Roentgen (1845–1923), to indicate that the exact nature of radiation is unknown.

(f) was first used by Paracelsus (1493–1541), with reference to air. In our modern sense, it was first used by the Belgian chemist Van Helmont (1577–1644), who said it is derived from the Greek *chaos*, "chaos."

(g) first appeared in a publication of 1886 by Nathan Birnbaum (1864–1937), writing under the pen name Martin Acher (*Selbst-Emancipation*, "self-emancipation").

(h) was introduced in 1941 by the physician Selman Abraham Waksman (born 1888), the discoverer of streptomycin.

(i) was coined in 1898 by a Scottish and an English chemist.

(j) was coined by the French philosopher and mathematician Blaise Pascal (1623–62).

(k) was coined in 1898 by the discoverers of this element (who also discovered neon), from the Greek for "hidden," because it took so long to find it.

(l) was G. B. Shaw's English translation of Nietzsche's *Übermensch*. (But the adjective *übermensch-lich*, "overhuman," had been in use in German since at least 1527, and was used by Herder and Goethe.)

(m) was coined, as a psychological term, by Neisser in 1906 (and popularized by Freud and Jung), from the Latin for "surrounding, embracing."

(n) was coined in 1888 by the German anatomist Wilhelm von Waldeyer-Hartz (1836–1921), from Greek words for "color" and "body."

(o) was first used in 1693 by the Dutch anatomist Verheyden when he dissected his own amputated leg.

(p) was coined in 1875 by the French engineer Clément Ader (1841–1925), from Latin for "bird."

(q) was coined by the French pathologist François-Boissier de la Croix de Sauvages (1706–67).

(r) was coined by the British medical writer James Braid (c. 1795–1860), from Greek for "sleep."

(s) was coined in 1817 by its inventor, Sir David Brewster (1781–1868), from Greek words for "beautiful" and "to see."

(t) was coined by the German physiologist K. F. Burdach (1776–1847).

(u) was coined by the French surgeon Sédillot in 1878, from Greek words for "small" and "life."

(v) was coined by the English poet Alexander Pope (1688–1744).

(w) was used, inadvertently, by the not very literate President W. G. Harding (1865–1923).

(x) was coined by the French aeronaut François Blanchard (1753–1809), meaning "stop the fall."

(y) was coined by the German biologist E. H. Haeckel (1834–1919), from the Greek for "house."

---

Correct answers: 1 (y), 2 (l), 3 (j), 4 (v), 5 (m), 6 (p), 7 (i), 8 (c), 9 (k), 10 (a), 11 (d), 12 (u), 13 (e), 14 (r), 15 (g), 16 (t), 17 (b), 18 (s), 19 (f), 20 (h), 21 (x), 22 (q), 23 (n), 24 (w), 25 (o)

Your score: _____
(25–21 correct: superb; 20–16 correct: good; 15–11 correct: fair)

# Vocabulary Test No. 17

Which word or phrase is nearest in meaning to each of the following headwords that are used in recounting the series of wars known as the Crusades (between the eleventh and the fourteenth centuries)?

1. shrine   (shrīn)
   (a) sharp, shrill cry or warning
   (b) receptacle for sacred relics
   (c) small, long-tailed crustacean, used as food
   (d) penultimate alcove in a mission house

2. caliph   (kal'if)
   (a) plant in Syria, with poisonous spikes
   (b) measuring stick, used originally to zero in on enemy emplacements
   (c) leader of Islam, claiming succession from Muhammad
   (d) bark from the cedars of Lebanon

3. pilgrim   (pil'grim)
   (a) one who flees religious persecution
   (b) rejuvenating herb found mainly along the Tigris River
   (c) person who journeys, as to some sacred place
   (d) point of no return at which the missionary continues on his way

4. corsair   (kôr'sâr)
   (a) vulture that fed on the Children's Crusades
   (b) prehistoric bird whose remains have been found in Palestine
   (c) two-headed pick for carving out Dead Sea scrolls
   (d) pirate or pirate vessel

5. infidel    (in'fid'l)
    (a) professed believer in Satan cults
    (b) person who has no religious faith
    (c) corps leader in the Crusades
    (d) lack of dignity

6. mercenary    (mûr'səner'ē)
    (a) woman who performs nursing without a license
    (b) euthanasia
    (c) soldier serving merely for money or other tangible reward
    (d) pretense or insincerity

7. schism    (siz'əm)
    (a) symbol of bird with ax in its beak
    (b) division into opposing factions because of disagreements
    (c) devious invasion of another land
    (d) vituperation

8. siege    (sēj)
    (a) prolonged and persistent period, as of illness
    (b) a type of earthquake
    (c) water in a moat
    (d) prophetess in Greece or Rome

9. preachy    (prē'chē)
    (a) infamous
    (b) present for an evening prayer service
    (c) silver-tongued
    (d) tediously and long-windedly instructive

10. deputation    (dep'yətā'shən)
    (a) vigorous interface
    (b) act of appointing an agent
    (c) derivation
    (d) path followed by the self-righteous

**Correct answers:** 1 (b), 2 (c), 3 (c), 4 (d), 5 (b), 6 (c), 7 (b), 8 (a), 9 (d), 10 (b)

**Your score:**_____
(10–9 correct: superb; 8–6 correct: good; 5–4 correct: fair)

# What Our Presidents Didn't Know

Which President—while he was in office—did not know this expression because it was coined or came into usage during the *next* administration? (See the example on page 42.)

1. tugboat: _____

2. mail chute: _____

3. Hoosier: _____

4. motorcycle: _____

5. kaleidoscope: _____

6. skywriting: _____

7. plastic: _____

8. cafeteria: _____

9. nitroglycerine: _____

10. poker: _____

_____

Correct answers: 1. James Monroe, 1817–25; 2. James Garfield, 1881; 3. John Quincy Adams, 1825–29; 4. Chester A. Arthur, 1881–85; 5. James Madison, 1809–17; 6. Woodrow Wilson, 1913–21; 7. William McKinley, 1897–1901; 8. Chester A. Arthur, 1881–85; 9. John Tyler, 1841–45; 10. John Quincy Adams, 1825–29

Your score:_____
(10–8 correct: superb; 7–4 correct: good; 3–2 correct: fair)

Which word or phrase is nearest in meaning to each of the following headwords, which are associated with politics?

1. **boondoggle**  (bōōn′dog′əl)
   - (a)  work of little value done merely to keep or look busy
   - (b)  backwoods or marsh
   - (c)  benefit greatly enjoyed
   - (d)  pound for stray pets

2. **infrastructure**  (in′frəstruk′chər)
   - (a)  ambiguity of Presidential campaigns
   - (b)  breach or violation, as of a law
   - (c)  the District of Columbia in its entirety
   - (d)  basic military installations and communication, of a country

3. **finesse**  (fines′)
   - (a)  deception or fraud
   - (b)  delicacy or subtlety in performance or skill
   - (c)  high finance
   - (d)  position papers in final form

4. **insurgent**  (insûr′jənt)
   - (a)  crest of a political tidal wave
   - (b)  rule of a kingdom of islands
   - (c)  person who rises up against established authority
   - (d)  politician's lead in preelection polling that is incapable of being surmounted

5. **sachem**  (sā′chəm)
   - (a)  chief of a nation among some American Indians
   - (b)  politico responsible for stabs in the back of a competitor
   - (c)  small bag containing payoff moneys
   - (d)  the act of pillaging

6. **curmudgeon** (kərmuj′ən)
   (a) official appointed for a specified period
   (b) irascible, churlish person
   (c) former mayor installed in an honorary position so that he can earn additional retirement benefits
   (d) signal to shout "the last hurrah"

7. **cant** (kant)
   (a) inability to perform
   (b) philosophical theory that power breeds greed and that greed breeds power
   (c) insincere statements, esp. pious platitudes
   (d) songlike and flowing style of oration

8. **mugwump** (mug′wump′)
   (a) person who is neutral on a controversial political issue
   (b) free canteen offered political followers
   (c) title of the first Dutch governors in the New World
   (d) self-seeking, servile flatterer

9. **to muckrake** (muk′rāk′)
   (a) to examine the sources of campaign contributions
   (b) to lay the groundwork for a Presidential run
   (c) to spread lies about other politicians
   (d) to search for and expose corruption, esp. in politics

10. **putsch** (pŏŏch)
   (a) mean, niggardly person with a penchant for saying the wrong things at the right time
   (b) revolt or uprising, esp. one that depends upon suddenness and speed
   (c) shady dealing on election day
   (d) demand by neophytes for a voice in their party's platform

---

Correct answers: 1 (a), 2 (d), 3 (b), 4 (c), 5 (a), 6 (b), 7 (c), 8 (a), 9 (d), 10 (b)

Your score:_____
(10–9 correct: superb; 8–6 correct: good; 5–4 correct: fair)

# Word Roots, Test F

Each of the following ten words stems from one of the three sources shown. Mark the correct answer.

1. villain
   (a) from Late Latin *villanus*, "farm laborer"
   (b) from Francisco ("Pancho") *Villa* (1877–1923)
   (c) from Latin *villosus*, "shaggy"

2. bandit
   (a) from Italian *bandito*, "proscribed"
   (b) from Old English *bana*, "slayer"
   (c) from Italian *banderuola*, "small banner"

3. riffraff
   (a) from Old French *rifler*, "to plunder"
   (b) from Old French *rif et raf*, "things of small value"
   (c) from the original punk-rock group of the same name, which is onomatopoeic

4. assassin
   (a) from Latin *asinus*, "ass"
   (b) from Latin *asseverare*, "to speak earnestly"
   (c) from Arabic *hashshashin*, "hashish eaters"

5. fiend
   (a) from Old English *feona*, "enemy"
   (b) from French *fer-de-lance*, "iron head of lance"
   (c) from Latin *ferus*, "savage"

6. blackmail
   (a) from *black* plus Middle English *maille*, "tribute"
   (b) from Old Norse *bladhra*, "to prattle"
   (c) from the name *Blakemore*

7. bunco
   (a) perhaps from Italian *banco*, "bank"
   (b) from *Buncombe* county in North Carolina
   (c) perhaps from Italian *bungnone*, "swelling"

8. aspersion
   (a) from Latin *asper*, "rough"
   (b) from Latin *aspirare*, "to breathe"
   (c) from Latin *aspersus*, "besprinkled"

9. pelf
   (a) from Old French *pelfre*, "booty"
   (b) from Greek *pelagos*, "sea"
   (c) from Latin *pelvis*, "basin"

10. duress
    (a) from Latin *duritia*, "hardness"
    (b) from Latin *duplex*, "twofold"
    (c) from Anglo-French *duete*, "that which is due"

---

Correct answers: 1 (a), 2 (a), 3 (b), 4 (c), 5 (a), 6 (a), 7 (a),
8 (c), 9 (a), 10 (a)

Your score:_____
(10–9 correct: superb; 8–6 correct: good; 5–4 correct: fair)

# I Seem To Be a Verb

## by R. Buckminster Fuller

I am quite confident that I invented the word *syntropy*. *Syntropy* because it seemed illogical to speak of "negative entropy"—*entropy* being already negative. Yet I wanted the opposite of *entropy*. All vegetation is *syntropic* as it photosynthetically converts the Sun's radiation into orderly hydrocarbon molecules.

I also know that I invented the phrase *Spaceship Earth*. Way back in 1956 I called it S.S. *Earth* as ships were called "S.S." from Steam Ship *Queen Elizabeth*, then I changed it to *Spaceship*.

*Dr. Fuller—a man of many words—was a comprehensive designer, inventor, engineer, mathematician, architect, cartographer, philosopher, poet, cosmogonist, choreographer, futurologist celebrated for developing geodesic houses that fly and dymaxion ways of living.*

# Chapter VII

## Vocabulary Test No. 19

Which word or phrase is nearest in meaning to each of the following headwords?

1. to kowtow   (kou'tou')
    (a) to walk on a path along which oxen towed river barges
    (b) to act in an obsequious manner
    (c) to measure the distance between Mars and Earth at their nearest point
    (d) to run off the rails of a track

2. mausoleum   (mô'səlē'əm)
    (a) little muscle (medicine)
    (b) meeting place of Southern gospel singers
    (c) stately and magnificent tomb built above ground
    (d) cabin of a Nile barge where queens like Cleopatra held court

3. Tory   (tōr'ē)
    (a) advocate of conservative principles
    (b) lightning rod
    (c) etiquette, usage, or fashion
    (d) twists, turns, or bends

4. to gerrymander   (jer'iman'dər)
    (a) to interfere with the successive changes of form from birth or hatching to adulthood in some animals, as of the pupa to the butterfly

- (b) to reject anything supernatural or incorporeal
- (c) to transpose letters, syllables, or sounds in a word
- (d) to divide (a state, country, etc.) into election districts so as to gain partisan advantage

5. **solecism** (sol'isiz'əm)
   - (a) breach of etiquette, or ungrammatical usage
   - (b) horrendous sunburn
   - (c) silence
   - (d) dignity, awe, or formality

6. **proletariat** (prō'litâr'ē·ət)
   - (a) supporters of a union
   - (b) the first to be singled out by foremen for overtime work
   - (c) the industrial working class
   - (d) cowboy with a gift for roping cattle

7. **billingsgate** (bil'iñgzgāt')
   - (a) coarsely or vulgarly abusive language
   - (b) man-size opening in a huge door at the entrance to a castle
   - (c) department-store invoices that must be paid by the tenth of a month or interest is added to the charge daily
   - (d) fishmongering

8. **sardonic** (särdon'ik)
   - (a) mockingly or tauntingly bitter
   - (b) pertaining to the red hat of a cardinal
   - (c) popular
   - (d) dancing

9. **Draconian** (drākō'nē·ən)
   - (a) believing in Greek gods
   - (b) dull
   - (c) rigorous, severe
   - (d) multitongued (esp. lizards)

98

10. to meander   (mē·an'dər)
    (a) to spout like a water geyser
    (b) to proceed by a winding or indirect course
    (c) to affect the relationship of parents to children
    (d) to subsist on cassava

---

Correct answers: 1 (b), 2 (c), 3 (a), 4 (d), 5 (a), 6 (c), 7 (a), 8 (a), 9 (c), 10 (b)

Your score:_____
(10–9 correct: superb; 8–6 correct: good; 5–4 correct: fair)

# New Kids on the Block

How well are you acquainted with some of the newly minted words and phrases? Indicate with "yes" or "no" whether you know the meaning. Then check the explanations.

1. D.H. burnout:_____
2. Twinkie defense:_____
3. digital roulette:_____
4. sex grab:_____
5. exchange exhaustion:_____
6. beam buff:_____
7. pulp guzzler:_____
8. mingles:_____
9. COLA:_____
10. uttering:_____
11. rubber room:_____
12. wetware:_____
13. the Ohs:_____
14. Six-Hour Retarded Child:_____
15. sequelitis:_____

Explanations:

1. *D.H. burnout:* Because of the designated-hitter rule in the American League—a dangerous slugger replaces the (usually) weak-hitting pitcher in the offensive lineup—A.L. pitchers are having to make a larger number of high-level, high-strain pitches per game and therefore are suffering more pain and disabling arm injuries than National League moundsmen.

**2.** *Twinkie defense:* The defense psychiatrist argues that the accused murderer overindulged in junk food, which led to bizarre, lethal behavior.

**3.** *digital roulette:* The hazard of dialing a wrong number increases as new area codes are established in a big city.

**4.** *sex grab:* A passer-by reaches for or actually touches the genitals or breast of a pedestrian.

**5.** *exchange exhaustion:* A telephone exchange, e.g., New York City's 212, literally runs out of numbers.

**6.** *beam buff:* an advocate of laser weapons in outer space

**7.** *pulp guzzler:* a big book (e.g., *Gone with the Wind*)

**8.** *mingles:* unmarried and unrelated persons living together

**9.** *COLA:* cost-of-*l*iving *a*djustment

**10.** *uttering:* passing counterfeit money or forged checks

**11.** *rubber room:* an office without work to do, esp. a government office

**12.** *wetware:* the human brain, correlating to software, which is the program, and hardware, which is the electronic equipment

**13.** *the Ohs:* This is what the decade after the 1990s may be called. Each year in the decade, which begins in 2001, has at least two *O*s in its name. (The Ohs, with a connotation of wonder—*The New York Times* has pointed out—would be fittingly optimistic for the start of a century.)

**14.** *Six-Hour Retarded Child* (according to the *Longman Dictionary of Psychology and Psychiatry*): "a child mistakenly judged to be retarded or a slow learner in school (for about six hours a day) while functioning well outside in a complex social world without any signs of retardation. This mistake— which often leads to a lifelong programing for failure—is made by middle-class teachers and psychologists who fail to realize that the child simply may not have middle-class habits such as sitting still and following instructions."

**15.** *sequelitis:* The actor takes the money and agrees to make still another (usually awful) movie like the one or two already made.

Your score: _____
(15–12 correct: superb; 11–9 correct: good; 8–7 correct: fair)

# Vocabulary Test No. 20

Which word or phrase is nearest in meaning to each of the following headwords?

1. **economy** (ikon'əmē)
   (a) branch of biology dealing with the relations between organisms and their environments
   (b) thrifty management of money, materials, etc.
   (c) balanced budget, government or personal
   (d) monetary farce played by people with money

2. **anarchy** (an'ərkē)
   (a) rule by monarch
   (b) state of society without government or law
   (c) winning of the seat of government by expert bowman
   (d) star field whose major points of light resemble a bowman

3. **to debauch** (dibôch')
   (a) to corrupt by sensuality, intemperance, etc.
   (b) to ignore
   (c) to set sail on German waters
   (d) to reduce in quality or value

4. **currency** (kûr'ənsē)
   (a) present-day version of an old idea
   (b) dog fight
   (c) any form of money that is circulated in a country
   (d) corporate bond unsecured by any mortgage

103

5. acolyte   (ak′əlīt′)
   (a) horrible figurehead extending from church roofs
   (b) altar attendant in public worship
   (c) disease of the sebaceous glands characterized esp.
       by pimples on the face that erupt in persons worried
       with money problems
   (d) torch at the entrance to Fort Knox

6. to palliate   (pal′ē·āt′)
   (a) to conceal the gravity of (an offense) by excuses
   (b) to feel unwell during a bear market
   (c) to wrap oneself in excuses for bad stock-market ad-
       vice
   (d) to pay off all debts with interest

7. conglomerate   (kən·glom′ərit)
   (a) goal of every American corporate executive whose
       principal concern is "the bottom line"
   (b) anything composed of heterogeneous elements
   (c) anything composed of homogeneous elements
   (d) major-domo of a corporation worth more than 3.75
       billion dollars

8. monopoly   (mənop′əlē)
   (a) paper profits
   (b) the corporate ideal
   (c) single product made by a small factory
   (d) exclusive privilege to carry on a business

9. hegemony   (hijem′ənē)
   (a) putting one's financial "eggs" into more than one
       stock portfolio
   (b) issuance of treasury bills
   (c) leadership or dominance, esp. of one nation over
       others
   (d) weekly money supply

10. liability   (lī′əbil′itē)
    (a) something disadvantageous
    (b) executive tergiversation
    (c) distinguished performance by a corporate executive
    (d) interest due on a long-term loan

**Correct answers:** 1 (b), 2 (b), 3 (a), 4 (c), 5 (b), 6 (a), 7 (b), 8 (d), 9 (c), 10 (a)

**Your score:**＿＿＿＿＿＿＿
(10–9 correct: superb; 8–6 correct: good; 5–4 correct: fair)

▓▓▓▓▓▓▓▓▓▓▓▓▓▓▓▓▓▓▓▓▓▓▓▓▓▓▓▓▓▓▓▓▓▓▓▓▓▓▓▓▓▓▓▓▓▓▓▓

# Fill In the Blanks

Example:
servilely compliant or deferential:
__ __ __equ __ __u __

The answer is "obsequious."

1. barren, miserable, unproductive in spite of great effort:
   __ __r d s c __ __b __ __ __

2. commandingly arrogant: i m p __ __ __o __ __

3. frivolously amusing: __a c e __ __o __ __

4. to accustom, as to a particular situation:
   __a b i __u __ __ __

5. the keeper or driver of an elephant in India:
   __ __h __u __

6. identification with or vicarious experiencing of the
   feelings or thoughts of another person:
   e __ __ __ __h __

7. a Spanish or Portuguese nobleman: __r a n d __ __

8. speaking or expressed in a lofty or pompous style:
   g r a n d __ __ __ __ __ __ __ __

9. to burst inward: i __ __ __ o d __

10. beginning to exist or develop: __a __ __ __n __

---

Correct answers: 1. hardscrabble 2. imperious 3. facetious 4.
habituate 5. mahout 6. empathy 7. grandee 8. grandiloquent
9. implode 10. nascent

Your score:_____
(10–9 correct: superb; 8–6 correct: good; 5–4 correct: fair)

# Vocabulary Test No. 21

Which word or phrase is nearest in meaning to each of the
following headwords, from the literature of the "man of the
century," the Nobel Prize-winning Winston Churchill?

1. crepuscular  (kripus′kyələr)
   (a) foolish, or half-witted
   (b) of or resembling twilight
   (c) painful
   (d) principal

2. coalition  (kō′əlish′ən)
   (a) community council
   (b) area containing coal deposits
   (c) assistant
   (d) alliance, esp. a temporary one between factions

3. mettle  (met′ʾl)
   (a) courage and fortitude
   (b) punishment
   (c) butting in
   (d) well-groomed couple

4. to blandish  (blan′dish)
   (a) to faint
   (b) to coax by cajolery
   (c) to be indifferent
   (d) to utter irreverent sayings about God or sacred things

5. abhorrent  (abhôr′ənt)
   (a) undergoing ablation
   (b) retracting solemnly
   (c) temporarily inactive
   (d) causing repugnance or loathing

6. **lodgment**   (loj′mənt)
   (a)   position gained from an enemy
   (b)   best seats for seeing ballet in rectangular hall
   (c)   rented quarters in another's house
   (d)   individualized form of expression

7. **unique**   (yo͞onēk′)
   (a)   outstanding, extraordinary
   (b)   inimitable
   (c)   existing as the sole example
   (d)   great

8. **equinoctial**   (ē′kwənok′shəl)
   (a)   pertaining to the celestial equator
   (b)   of even weight
   (c)   in the first line of defense (on a beach)
   (d)   heavily protected and secret in location

9. **insuperable**   (inso͞o′pərəbəl)
   (a)   not endurable or bearable
   (b)   not to be overcome or surmounted
   (c)   not covered by insurance
   (d)   not distinguished

10. **dauntless**   (dônt′lis)
   (a)   without male heir
   (b)   protective
   (c)   not to be discouraged
   (d)   trifling

---

Correct answers: 1 (b), 2 (d), 3 (a), 4 (b), 5 (d), 6 (a), 7 (c), 8 (a), 9 (b), 10 (c)

Your score:_____
(10–9 correct: superb; 8–6 correct: good; 5–4 correct: fair)

# Word Roots, Test G

Each of the following ten words stems from one of the three sources shown. Mark the correct answer.

1. **gadfly**
   (a) from Middle English *gad*, "goad"
   (b) from *gad*, a euphemism for *God*
   (c) coined by Sir Isaac Walton (the literate fisherman), of unknown derivation

2. **belladonna**
   (a) from Old English *belig*, "bag"
   (b) from Italian *bella donna*, "fair lady"
   (c) from Latin *bellum*, "war"

3. **dandelion**
   (a) from Latin *damascenum*, "(plum) of Damascus"
   (b) from Middle French *dent de lion*, "lion's tooth"
   (c) from Old French *dangier*, "danger"

4. **brontosaur**
   (a) from *Brontes*, one of the Cyclopes in Greek mythology
   (b) from Greek *bronte*, "thunder," plus *sauros*, "lizard"
   (c) from the name of the hideous-looking *Brontë* parsonage in West Riding of Yorkshire

5. **armadillo**
   (a) from the Biblical *Armageddon*, the great final battle to take place at the end of the world
   (b) from Latin *armilla*, "bracelet"
   (c) from the Spanish diminutive of *armadado*, "armed"

109

6. **dromedary**
   - (a) from Greek *dromas*, "running"
   - (b) from Middle French *drolle*, "scamp"
   - (c) from Greek *kamelos*, "camel"

7. **dodo**
   - (a) from Portuguese *doudo*, "silly"
   - (b) from Old English *docga*, "dog"
   - (c) reduplication of *doe*

8. **lemur**
   - (a) from Latin *lemures*, "ghosts"
   - (b) from *Lemoore*, a town in California
   - (c) from Middle English *lemman*, "sweetheart"

9. **scavenger**
   - (a) from Greek *skatos*, "dung"
   - (b) from Persian *saqalat*, "scarlet cloth"
   - (c) from Anglo-French *scawager*, "inspector"

10. **tulip**
    - (a) from *Tulle*, a city in France
    - (b) from Turkish *tulbend*, "turban"
    - (c) from Old English *toth*, "tooth"

---

Correct answers: 1 (a), 2 (b), 3 (b), 4 (b), 5 (c), 6 (a), 7 (a), 8 (a), 9 (c), 10 (b)

Your score:_____
(10–9 correct: superb; 8–6 correct: good; 5–4 correct: fair)

# Like Gag Me with a Spoon!

## by James Sledd

To lots of people who make their living by worrying publicly about other people's English, *finalize* is an abomination. It is, says E. B. White, "a peculiarly fuzzy and silly word. Does it mean 'terminate,' or does it mean 'put into final form'? One can't be sure, really, what it means, and one gets the impression that the person using it doesn't know, either, and doesn't want to know" (Strunk and White, *The Elements of Style*, 3d edition, page 83). When J.F.K. told a questioner, "We haven't finalized any plans," *The New York Times* was moved to emit a smart-ass editorial. Eisenhower must have "left a few loose words" lying around the White House, the editorial said (November 30, 1961), and Kennedy must have picked them up.

A better informed editorial-writer would have known that his own paper had used *finalization* way back in 1952 and that the old Thunderer itself, the *Times* of London, had used *finalized* six years before Kennedy did (*A Supplement to the Oxford English Dictionary*, Vol. I, s.v. *finalize*). What's *wrong* with using it? *Finalize* is formed by adding the suffix *-ize* (*-ise* if you're a limey) to the adjective *final*, just like *actualize*, *brutalize*, *centralize*, *decimalize*, *equalize*, *formalize*, *generalize*, and so on through the alphabet; it's been used for at least sixty years now, and always by people with some claim to education; its handful of meanings are understandably related (many words have far more) and are certainly no more confusing than those of *rationalize* or *socialize*; it doesn't just duplicate an already existing word, as a made-up *historicalize* would duplicate *historicize*; and in fact it's hard to think of an equally useful synonym. For example, when an official *finalizes* reports that have been prepared by his staff, he isn't *finishing* those reports; he's giving them his final approval. In the same way, when one country *finalizes* a break with another, their hostility isn't finished but only well begun. The resultant shoot-out might finish but not *finalize* the citizens of both.

111

So how can we generalize and moralize from *finalize*? We all have the right to be as finicky as we please about our own words and sentences. I personally don't use *contact* as a verb because my father insisted that *contact* is a noun; and since the dean of my college quite unreasonably got after me when I was an undergraduate fifty years ago, I haven't begun one sentence with *however* meaning "nevertheless." A resolute if not very successful fisherman, I've never learned, either, to fish with a *spinning reel*. I don't refuse, however (*that's* where the word belongs!), to eat the trout that my *spinning sons* provide me, and I don't *barf* when my *grotty* students (they spell it grody) forget that *convince* takes a clause with "that" and not an infinitive. We're using language, that is to say, when we read and listen as well as when we speak and write, and we're *misusing* it when we try to impose our own irrational preferences on other people. English today is the closest thing we have to a universal language. Like gag me with a spoon! A language for the whole world must be adaptable to the whole world's needs.

*Dr. Sledd is Professor of English at the University of Texas.*

# Chapter VIII

## Vocabulary Test No. 22

Which word or phrase is nearest in meaning to each of the following headwords?

1. libertine (lib′ərtēn′)
   (a) chief justice of a nation
   (b) person trained for and engaged in library service
   (c) person who maintains the doctrine of free will
   (d) person who is morally or sexually unrestrained

2. approbation (ap′rəbā′shən)
   (a) approval, esp. by authority
   (b) money authorized to be paid for a special purpose
   (c) creation for use
   (d) small body, often a remnant of a comet, that strikes the Earth

3. licit (lis′it)
   (a) not permitted by law
   (b) permitted by law
   (c) full of lust
   (d) restrained

4. to usurp (yōōsûrp′)
   (a) to inhabit
   (b) to abort
   (c) to seize and hold without legal right
   (d) to put to practical or beneficial use

113

5. **probity**   (prō′bitē)
   (a) integrity and uprightness
   (b) group of subordinates or attendants of a high-rank-
       ing person
   (c) abundance
   (d) medical examination in connection with a murder

6. **nepotism**   (nep′ətiz′əm)
   (a) paralysis of the nervous system
   (b) favoritism on the basis of family relationship
   (c) unattractiveness
   (d) the throwing of dice to determine ranking in a po-
       litical unit

7. **venal**   (vēn′ᵊl)
   (a) commanding respect because of great age or asso-
       ciated dignity
   (b) bloody
   (c) wishful
   (d) open to bribery

8. **pettifogger**   (pet′ēfog′ər)
   (a) shifty and sometimes dishonest lawyer
   (b) idealist
   (c) cynic
   (d) pessimist

9. **iniquity**   (inik′witē)
   (a) dishonest reporting
   (b) hostility
   (c) gross injustice
   (d) memory gap

10. **specious**   (spē′shəs)
    (a) unjustified
    (b) apparently good or right but lacking real merit
    (c) criminal but pretending to act in the public interest
    (d) mendacious in the witness box before a judge and
        jury

**Correct answers:** 1 (d), 2 (a), 3 (b), 4 (c), 5 (a), 6 (b), 7 (d), 8 (a), 9 (c), 10 (b)

**Your score:** _____
(10–9 correct: superb; 8–6 correct: good; 5–4 correct: fair)

# Scramblings

Each phrase defines the word that follows it in scrambled form. Can you put the eggs back together again?

Example:
wise and discerning: eiastpn _____

The answer is "sapient."

1. the result obtained by dividing one number into another: ueiqtnot _____

2. the exaltation of a person to the rank of a god; a deified or glorified ideal: oashseipto _____

3. beyond ordinary knowledge or understanding; little known or obscure: etidnocer _____

4. the killing of a king; a person who kills a king: giierdec _____

5. mere nonsense; a flimsy trifle: llorofed _____

6. the first five books of the Old Testament: nthcepeuat _____

7. of or supported by gifts or charity: yranysomeele _____

8. twilight or dusk: gngoamil _____

9. a word opposite in meaning to another: tnynmoa _____

10. feeble in mind; irresponsible and careless: lkcssefe _____

**Correct answers:** 1. quotient 2. apotheosis 3. recondite 4. regicide 5. folderol 6. Pentateuch 7. eleemosynary 8. gloaming 9. antonym 10. feckless

**Your score:** _____
(10–9 correct: superb; 8–6 correct: good; 5–4 correct: fair)

# Vocabulary Test No. 23

Which word or phrase is nearest in meaning to each of the following headwords that are rooted in antiquity?

1. to vulcanize (vul'kəniz')
   (a) to erupt like clockwork
   (b) to fizzle in a test tube, then evaporate
   (c) to treat (rubber) under heat with sulfur to make it more durable
   (d) to synchronize

2. euphemism (yōō'fəmiz'əm)
   (a) scarcely perceptible difference
   (b) castrated man, esp. formerly one employed by Oriental rulers as a harem attendant
   (c) exclamation of triumph at a discovery
   (d) substitution of a mild or vague expression for one thought to be offensive

3. Stygian (stij'ē·ən)
   (a) causing a pink coloration in the eye
   (b) sewn together
   (c) dark or gloomy; infernal; hellish
   (d) pertaining to a liquid that polymerizes to a transparent material

4. Cyclopean (sī'kləpē'ən)
   (a) gigantic, vast (like Cyclops, a giant with a single round eye in the middle of the forehead)
   (b) recurring with regularity
   (c) exclusive of the nucleus of a cell
   (d) referring to the machine that helped to decipher the Trojan code before Actium

5. amorphous (əmôr'fəs)
   (a) containing solutions for hypodermic injection
   (b) living on land and water

118

(c) lacking definite form
(d) one-celled

6. **Elysium** (ilizh′ē·əm)
   (a) image that can be distorted when seen with only one eye
   (b) well-educated or aristocratic man
   (c) place or state of perfect happiness
   (d) place where the Greeks' most famous dramatists exhibited their plays

7. **Saturnalia** (sat′ərnā′lē·a)
   (a) cultural event that climaxes the week
   (b) band of ivory rings on the neck of an Ibi princess
   (c) cheap, small-caliber handgun that is easily obtainable
   (d) period of unrestrained revelry

8. **microcosm** (mī′krəkoz′əm)
   (a) sore throat caused by postnasal drip
   (b) miniature
   (c) unleavened bread on the Passover table
   (d) college course requiring little effort

9. **medusa** (mədōō′sə)
   (a) jellyfish
   (b) ear ache
   (c) soft, marrowlike center of an organ
   (d) reward or recompense

10. **calliope** (kalī′əpē)
    (a) the white lily now growing only in Hollywood
    (b) musical instrument consisting of a set of harsh-sounding steam whistles which are activated by a keyboard
    (c) the art of beautiful handwriting
    (d) callous condition

---

Correct answers: 1 (c), 2 (d), 3 (c), 4 (a), 5 (c), 6 (c), 7 (d), 8 (b), 9 (a), 10 (b)

Your score: _____
(10–9 correct: superb; 8–6 correct: good; 5–4 correct: fair)

# There *Is* a Word for It

Example:
a group of subordinates or attendants of a high-ranking person: r _____ .

The answer is "retinue."

1. a mayonnaise dressing with chopped pickles, onions, olives, etc.:
   t _____    s _____

2. a set of three panels side by side, bearing pictures or carvings, often used as an altarpiece:
   t _____

3. a rustling, as of silk; elaborate decoration, esp. on women's clothing: f _____

4. an Arab sailing vessel common on the Arabian and Indian coasts, generally having two or three masts:
   d _____

5. an edible European flatfish with a diamond-shaped body:
   t _____

6. a man's wig of the seventeenth and eighteenth centuries:
   p _____

7. to be fretfully discontented: r _____ .

8. a class of persons making their way on their own ability and talent rather than because of class privileges:
   m _____

9. the title of the Turkish viceroys in Egypt from 1867 to 1914:

   k _____

10. to grind into coarse particles: k _____

_____

**Correct answers: 1.** tartar sauce **2.** triptych **3.** froufrou **4.** dhow **5.** turbot **6.** peruke **7.** repine **8.** meritocracy **9.** khedive **10.** kibble

**Your score:** _____
(10–9 correct: superb; 8–6 correct: good; 5–4 correct: fair)

# Vocabulary Test No. 24

Which word or phrase is nearest in meaning to each of the following headwords?

1. mercurial    (mərkyŏŏr'ē·əl)
   (a) forgiving
   (b) changeable and erratic in mood
   (c) entitled to reward or commendation
   (d) merry

2. pernicious    (pərnish'əs)
   (a) granting permission
   (b) busily walking or traveling about, esp. on assignment
   (c) unwelcome
   (d) causing insidious harm or ruin

3. to scud    (skud)
   (a) to gallop
   (b) to run or move quickly
   (c) to collect dirt from the gutter
   (d) to sink

4. cadence    (kād'ᵊns)
   (a) rhythmic flow of language
   (b) composition with one or more instruments with orchestral accompaniment
   (c) shrill, broken sound of a hen
   (d) man who behaves crudely toward women

5. quiescent    (kwē·es'ənt)
   (a) unemployed
   (b) in debt
   (c) at rest or quiet
   (d) in slight but rapid motion

6. **stagnant**   (stag'nənt)
   - (a) sluggish or dull
   - (b) going it alone
   - (c) flighty and capricious
   - (d) not accompanied by a female companion


7. **sedentary**   (sed'ᵊnter'ē)
   - (a) sullied
   - (b) intrepid
   - (c) fertilizing
   - (d) characterized by much sitting and little physical activity


8. **nomad**   (nō'mad)
   - (a) wanderer
   - (b) a catatonic
   - (c) one who has sunk to a lower level
   - (d) patriarch who commands an ark


9. **motile**   (mō'til)
   - (a) built near a highway
   - (b) powered by a small and powerful engine, esp. an internal-combustion engine
   - (c) capable of moving spontaneously
   - (d) exhibiting great diversity of elements


10. **peregrination**   (per'əgrənā'shən)
    - (a) the act of rescuing
    - (b) redundancy
    - (c) international diplomacy
    - (d) long journey or wandering

---

Correct answers: **1** (b), **2** (d), **3** (b), **4** (a), **5** (c), **6** (a), **7** (d), **8** (a), **9** (c), **10** (d)

Your score:_____
(10–9 correct: superb; 8–6 correct: good; 5–4 correct: fair)

# Word Roots, Test H

Each of the following ten words stems from one of the three sources shown. Mark the correct answer.

1. chop suey
   (a) from pidgin English *chop*, "fast"
   (b) from Chinese *chow chow* (a breed of dog)
   (c) from Cantonese *shap sui*, "odds and ends"

2. sherbet
   (a) from Persian *shah*, "king"
   (b) from Persian *sharbat*, "beverage"
   (c) from Old English *scearu*, "division"

3. relish
   (a) from Middle French *relier*, "to bind"
   (b) from Old French *reles*, "aftertaste"
   (c) from Latin *reliquus*, "remaining"

4. cookie
   (a) from Latin *coquus*, "cook"
   (b) from the slang word *cooky*
   (c) from Dutch *koekje*, "little cake"

5. kipper
   (a) from Icelandic *kippa*, "bundle"
   (b) from Old English *cypera*, "spawning salmon"
   (c) from Arabic *qismat*, "destiny"

6. chowder
   (a) from French *chaudière*, "kettle"
   (b) from *Chowchilla*, a town in California
   (c) from Chinese *chow mein*, "fried dough"

124

7. **canteen**
   - (a) from Italian *cantina*, "cellar"
   - (b) from Middle French *canton*, "corner"
   - (c) from Hawaiian *kanaka*, "man"

8. **banquet**
   - (a) from Irish *bean sidhe*, "fairy woman"
   - (b) from Italian *banchetto*, "small bench"
   - (c) from the feast celebrated by Macbeth and *Banquo*

9. **bib**
   - (a) from Greek *biblia*, "books"
   - (b) from Middle English *bibben*, "to drink"
   - (c) from Old English *biddan*, "to beg"

10. **Capricorn**
    - (a) from Italian *capriccio*, "caprice"
    - (b) from Latin *caper*, "goat," plus *cornu*, "horn"
    - (c) from Latin *capito*, "big head"

---

Correct answers: 1 (c), 2 (b), 3 (b), 4 (c), 5 (b), 6 (a), 7 (a), 8 (b), 9 (b), 10 (b)

Your score:_____
(10–9 correct: superb; 8–6 correct: good; 5–4 correct: fair)

# Mumpsimus

### by John B. Bremner

A young priest once (in 1517) corrected an old priest for saying *mumpsimus* instead of *sumpsimus* ("we have received") in the first prayer after Communion in the Latin Mass. "Son," said the old priest—or so the story goes—"I've been saying *mumpsimus* for thirty years and I'm not going to change my old *mumpsimus* for your new *sumpsimus*."

Though not often heard these days, *mumpsimus* has been in the language for more than four hundred years. It means: (1) an error, usually caused by ignorance, long embedded in language or in life; (2) obstinate adherence to the error after correction; and (3) a person who insists on perpetuating the error.

*Mumpsimus*, says Noah Jonathan Jacobs, in *Naming-Day in Eden*, is "a much needed word to describe an unlovely trait in human nature that, because of the force of habit, or the sin of pride, resents the intimation that the first impression we form stands in need of revision." Jacobs regrets that *mumpsimus* is no longer in common use. Amen.

*Dr. Bremner is Stauffer Professor of Journalism at the University of Kansas, and the author of* Words on Words.

# Chapter IX

## Vocabulary Test No. 25

Which word or phrase is nearest in meaning today to each of the following headwords from the quill of William Shakespeare?

1. bastinado    (bas'tənā'dō)
    (a) a beating with a stick, cudgel, etc.
    (b) illegitimate offspring
    (c) strong woody fiber used in cordage
    (d) utensil of bamboo

2. to beseech    (bisēch')
    (a) to look sharply
    (b) to expectorate
    (c) to catch in or as in a trap
    (d) to beg or ask eagerly

3. precipice    (pres'əpis)
    (a) sudden death
    (b) cliff with a vertical face
    (c) concise summary
    (d) scrupulousness

4. malignant    (məlig'nənt)
    (a) taking on the form of gossip
    (b) disposed to cause harm
    (c) pretending illness in order to avoid duty
    (d) gentle

5. changeling   (ch̲ānj′li̅n̲g)
   (a) child surreptitiously or unintentionally substituted for another
   (b) surgery that removes a thinking part of the brain
   (c) menopause
   (d) coinage

6. whelk   (hwelk)
   (a) a blow across the shoulders
   (b) large, edible marine mollusk with a spiral-shaped shell
   (c) yelp of a dog
   (d) watery liquid that separates from milk after it curdles

7. antipodes   (antip′ədēz′)
   (a) places diametrically opposite to each other on the globe
   (b) twin tadpoles developed in scientific experiments
   (c) antiparticles
   (d) Spanish beans

8. knave   (nāv)
   (a) unprincipled or dishonest person
   (b) artless, ingenuous, unsophisticated young man
   (c) child's nursemaid (Brit.)
   (d) female goat

9. wanton   (won′t°n)
   (a) desirous
   (b) scheming
   (c) sickly pale or ashen
   (d) malicious and unjustifiable

10. potation   (pōtā′sh̲ən)
    (a) fleshy oblong or rounded outgrowth of an underground stem
    (b) the act of drinking
    (c) soft, moist mass of herbs, etc., spread on a cloth and applied as a medicament to the body
    (d) food that happens to be available without special preparation

Correct answers: 1 (a), 2 (d), 3 (b), 4 (b), 5 (a), 6 (a), 7 (a), 8 (a), 9 (d), 10 (b)

Your score: _____
(10–9 correct: superb; 8–6 correct: good; 5–4 correct: fair)

# State the Name!

Do you know how each of the fifty states got its name?

1. Alabama _____
    (a) renamed for Governor George Wallace's mother
    (b) from the name of an Indian tribe: "here we rest"
    (c) from a popular song by Kurt Weill

2. Alaska _____
    (a) from the Eskimo word for "the far country"
    (b) from Russian for "over the sea"
    (c) from the Aleut word *alyeska*, "the great land," "the main land"

3. Arizona _____
    (a) from the Indian word *arizonac*, "little spring"
    (b) from Pueblo for "beautiful sunset"
    (c) the title of a sixteenth-century Spanish play, the first performed in the New World, in Santa Fe

4. Arkansas _____
    (a) a word made up by Noah Noah, an evangelist
    (b) the original name for Dorothy Gale's home
    (c) from the name of the *Arkansas* Indians: "downstream people"

**5. California** _____

    (a) Indian word for "gold in these here hills"

    (b) probably from Queen *Calafia*, ruler over a fabulous country in a book by Garci Ordonez de Montalvo, *Las Sergas de Esplandian*

    (c) named by Francis Drake for Elizabeth I's bastard daughter

**6. Colorado** _____

    (a) named for the *Colorado* River; Spanish, "red" or "ruddy"

    (b) picked by Francisco Vasquez de *Coronado* from a list provided by Queen Isabella

    (c) English for *Coronado*

**7. Connecticut** _____

    (a) unknown to this day

    (b) from a word play in Shakespeare's *The Winter's Tale*

    (c) from the Indian word *quinnehtukqut*, "beside the long tidal river"

**8. Delaware** _____

    (a) named for the first baby born in the New World, *Della Ware*

    (b) named for Lord *de la Warr*, the first governor of Virginia

    (c) suggested by Peter Minuet, who founded New Sweden, near today's Wilmington

**9. Florida** _____

    (a) Spanish for "flowery, full of flowers"; named by Ponce de León when he discovered this land on Easter Sunday (*Pascua florida*, "flowery Easter") in 1513

131

(b) coined by Columbus to honor his teenage daughter who died on his third voyage across the Great Ocean Sea

(c) named for the Seminole *Floridete*, who then nearly killed Andrew Jackson

10. Georgia _____

(a) derived from *gorge*

(b) Thomas More's obverse name for Utopia

(c) named for *George* II of England, who had granted the charter to the colony in 1732

11. Hawaii _____

(a) named by the traditional discoverer of the islands, *Hawaii Loa*, after himself (one of the various explanations of the name)

(b) the title of the popular song by the Hawaiian queen who wrote many "pineapples," as golden oldies were called in the mid-nineteenth century

(c) from the Earl of Sandwich's favorite appetizer, now known as chopped liver

12. Idaho _____

(a) from Sioux, for "hot potato"

(b) from the Shoshoni Indian words *ee dah how*, "the sun comes down the mountain"

(c) named for the first Oriental woman to bear a daughter there, *Ida W. Ho*

13. Illinois _____

(a) from the name of the *Illini* Indians—the French rendition of *iliniwek*, "men"

132

(b) named for a Yale president, famous for his pioneering spirit

(c) preferred to the original name by settlers made ill by polluted waters

14. Indiana _____

(a) the title of a haunting ode by Longfellow

(b) named by Lewis and Clark after spending a fortnight with *Indian* squaws

(c) meaning simply "Land of the *Indians*"

15. Iowa _____

(a) winning submission, by Billy Sunday, in Dubuque *Register* contest

(b) from an Indian word meaning "this is the place"

(c) from Sioux for "stay awhile"

16. Kansas _____

(a) literally *can saw*, a French-Canadian sobriquet

(b) from the name of the *Kansa* or *Kaw* Indians: "people of the south wind"

(c) once *Sas*, extended by an Indian hunter named Adam who hated palindromes

17. Kentucky _____

(a) named for the *Kentucky* River; probably from the Iroquois Indian word *ken-tah-ten*, "land of tomorrow"

(b) Lord Byron's name for Daniel Boone's forest home, in 1818 poem

(c) probably from "American" for the Cherokee "beyond the blue"

133

18. Louisiana _____

(a) named for *Louise Anna*, the most renowned brothel operator in the delta in the seventeenth century

(b) Marquis de Lafayette's mother's maiden name

(c) named for *Louis* XIV and his mother, *Anne* of Austria (Louis-i-Ane), by Robert Cavalier de la Salle in 1682

19. Maine _____

(a) originally the Spanish *Maino*, now Americanized

(b) named *The Main* by sailors, in contrast to the many islands

(c) named by the great-grandfather of R. Buckminster Fuller, for the "chance" for greatness that he foresaw in his heirs

20. Maryland _____

(a) named for Henrietta *Maria*, Queen of England, wife of Charles I

(b) named for Lord *Maryland*, cousin of Lord Baltimore

(c) originally *Merry Land*, changed by the second wave of Catholic settlers

21. Massachusetts _____

(a) from Abenaki for "freedom's land"

(b) from the name of the *Massachusetts* Indians: "great mountain place" or "great hill's mouth"

(c) from the name of the *Massachusetts* Indians: "only trouble"

134

22. Michigan _____
    (a) from Huron for "shooting star," which reportedly struck the area like a nuclear explosion

    (b) named for Lake *Michigan*; from the Indian word *michiguma*, "god water"

    (c) family name of a Pennsylvania Dutchman who claimed the region for "other brave souls"

23. Minnesota _____
    (a) from the Dakota Indian word *minisota*, "sky-tinted waters"

    (b) a more pronounceable version of *Minnehahahaha"*

    (c) Indian (Huron) for the Spanish explorer Hernando *de Soto*, who discovered the Mississippi

24. Mississippi _____
    (a) same origin as *Missouri*

    (b) from French for "the river of the universe"

    (c) of unknown origin; generally assumed to come from an Indian word meaning "father of waters"

25. Missouri _____
    (a) from Apache for "uncontrollable waters"

    (b) named for the *Missouri* River; from an Indian word meaning "the people of the long boats"

    (c) favored by *Sooners*, whose *misery* earned company, thus eventually *Missouri*

26. Montana _____
    (a) Spanish for "mountainous"

    (b) named for the sister of Louise Anna (see Louisiana)

(c) Russian for "barren, nothing doing"

27. Nebraska _____

(a) from the Omaha Indian word *nibthaska*, "flat water"

(b) from the Omaha Indian word *nibthaska*, "funny place"

(c) name of Geronimo's third wife and second daughter

28. Nevada _____

(a) from Chinese for "break pick," on railroad work

(b) from Chinese for "Union Pacific"

(c) Spanish for "snow-clad" or "snow capped"

29. New Hampshire _____

(a) from Iroquois for "white mountains"

(b) named by John Mason, in the 1600s, after *Hampshire*, his own county in England

(c) once *New York-Hamp*, renamed after Ethan Allen severed the region

30. New Jersey _____

(a) named by William Shakespeare, at the behest of a patron returned from the New World

(b) named for the new kind of *Jersey* cow nurtured there

(c) named by Sir George Carteret for his birthplace, the island of *Jersey* in the English Channel

31. New Mexico _____

(a) translation of the earlier Spanish *Nuevo Mexico*

(b) once known as *Olde Mexico*, and renamed after the battle of the Alamo

(c) renamed when its original designation proved embarrassing in English translation

32. New York _____

(a) named for the Duke of *York*, who became King James II

(b) named by Sephardic Jewish immigrants from Brazil, in 1576

(c) from *Hamlet*, "Alas, poor *Yorick*! I *knew* him, Horatio."

33. North Carolina _____

(a) originally *South Carolina*, until Mason and Dixon, cartographers, set it straight

(b) named for *Charles* I of England; originally spelled *Carolana*

(c) named for a sister of Charles I of England, *Caroline O'Carolina*, of Northumbrage

34. North Dakota _____

(a) coined by Bat Masterson, cowboy term for "bad lands"

(b) from an Indian word meaning "allies"

(c) "north" plus an Indian word meaning "(white man) go away."

35. Ohio _____

(a) named for the *Ohio* River; from an Iroquois Indian word that was used to show that something was big

(b) from a word of the mounds people for "wigwam"

(c) from the original Irish name *O'Hiog*, altered by the Know-Nothing Party and by Act of Congress (1855)

36. Oklahoma _____

    (a) named for *Okies*, first settlers

    (b) from two Choctaw Indian words, *okla*, "people," and *homa*, "red"

    (c) from three Choctaw Indian words for "better sooner later"

37. Oregon _____

    (a) chosen by referendum in 1843 over *Salmonton*

    (b) named in honor of the first pioneer woman to reach what is now the *Oregon* River (1838)

    (c) named for the *Oregon* River; probably an Indian word

38. Pennsylvania _____

    (a) not named for its founder, William *Penn*, but for his father, Admiral William *Penn*: "Penn's wood"

    (b) Latin for "nymphs of the trees"

    (c) Latin for "marked land," or "keystone"

39. Rhode Island _____

    (a) renamed for the English magnate *Rhodes*, whose gift of $4.6 million restored the state treasury to the Constitutionally-mandated surplus

    (b) twin of Meadow Island preferred by voters

    (c) named for the Greek island of Rhodes—perhaps because someone found resemblances (The official name of the state is "State of Rhode Island and Providence Plantations.")

40. South Carolina _____

    (a) selected by Constitutional Convention after area split away from *North Carolina*

(b) same origin as *North Carolina*

(c) originally owned by *Carroll Carroll*, oldest-lived signer of the Declaration of Independence, and named for his daughter, *Sue Caroline*

41. South Dakota ____ (a) from Chinkook for "sky loves red earth"

(b) named for a baby dinosaur first discovered here, plus *South*

(c) same origin as *North Dakota*

42. Tennessee ____ (a) from the Greek for "long view"

(b) named for the *Tennessee* River; an Indian word of unknown meaning

(c) from German for "much food"

43. Texas ____ (a) from the Caddo Indian word *tejas*, "friends" or "allies"

(b) named by Samuel Houston, an English teacher who stressed similes

(c) from Spanish *Texasado*, "as far as the eye can see"

44. Utah ____ (a) originally *Youtah*, Iroquois for "young place"

(b) from the name of the *Ute* Indians: "hill dwellers"

(c) from a Ute Indian verb for "to rattle and shake" (The area suffered much earthquake damage in the early 1800s.)

45. Vermont ____ (a) named by Ethan and Ira Allen for their father's estate near Paris

(b) from an Abenaki Indian word for "clear waters"

(c) from French *Ver Mont*, "green mountain"

46. Virginia \_\_\_\_\_

(a) named for Queen Elizabeth I, the *Virgin Queen*

(b) named for *Virginia* Dare, first English baby born in New World

(c) named for what the area didn't have after arrivals had spent seven, nearly eight, weeks at sea, in the 1520s

47. Washington \_\_\_\_\_

(a) named for George *Washington's* second son

(b) originally from a Chinese pejorative, *ton* later replacing the suffix to prevent embarrassment

(c) named in honor of George *Washington*

48. West Virginia \_\_\_\_\_

(a) named in honor of Lady *West*, the *Virgin Queen*'s favorite lady-in-waiting

(b) same origin as *Virginia*

(c) named for a queen of the Iroquois Confederation

49. Wisconsin \_\_\_\_\_

(a) from the Menomonee Indian word *wiskosspeo*, with uncertain meaning (Until 1836, the name of the territory was *Wiskonsan*.)

(b) from the Creek Indian word *whistofthemoon*, "northern lights"

(c) from a local word, of unknown origin, for "cow cheese"

50. Wyoming _____

(a) named for an Indian, "best friend" of Speaker of the House Hull, in the 1870s

(b) from the Delaware Indian word *meche-weami-ing*, "at the big flats"

(c) unknown to this day

**Correct answers:**

| | | | |
|---|---|---|---|
| 1 (Alabama) | (b) | 26 (Montana) | (a) |
| 2 (Alaska) | (c) | 27 (Nebraska) | (a) |
| 3 (Arizona) | (a) | 28 (Nevada) | (c) |
| 4 (Arkansas) | (c) | 29 (New Hampshire) | (b) |
| 5 (California) | (b) | 30 (New Jersey) | (c) |
| 6 (Colorado) | (a) | 31 (New Mexico) | (a) |
| 7 (Connecticut) | (c) | 32 (New York) | (a) |
| 8 (Delaware) | (b) | 33 (North Carolina) | (b) |
| 9 (Florida) | (a) | 34 (North Dakota) | (b) |
| 10 (Georgia) | (c) | 35 (Ohio) | (a) |
| 11 (Hawaii) | (a) | 36 (Oklahoma) | (b) |
| 12 (Idaho) | (b) | 37 (Oregon) | (c) |
| 13 (Illinois) | (a) | 38 (Pennsylvania) | (a) |
| 14 (Indiana) | (c) | 39 (Rhode Island) | (c) |
| 15 (Iowa) | (b) | 40 (South Carolina) | (b) |
| 16 (Kansas) | (b) | 41 (South Dakota) | (c) |
| 17 (Kentucky) | (a) | 42 (Tennessee) | (b) |
| 18 (Louisiana) | (c) | 43 (Texas) | (a) |
| 19 (Maine) | (b) | 44 (Utah) | (b) |
| 20 (Maryland) | (a) | 45 (Vermont) | (c) |
| 21 (Massachusetts) | (b) | 46 (Virginia) | (a) |
| 22 (Michigan) | (b) | 47 (Washington) | (c) |
| 23 (Minnesota) | (a) | 48 (West Virginia) | (b) |
| 24 (Mississippi) | (c) | 49 (Wisconsin) | (a) |
| 25 (Missouri) | (b) | 50 (Wyoming) | (b) |

Your score: _____
(50–41 correct: superb; 40–31 correct: good; 30–21 correct: fair)

# Vocabulary Test No. 26

Which word or phrase is nearest in meaning to each of the following headwords, which were used by the "button-cute, wafer-thin" humorist S. J. Perelman?

1. turgid (tûr′jid)
    (a) having a diamond-shaped body
    (b) unduly distended or swollen
    (c) cleansing
    (d) inhabiting tropical and temperate America

2. ne′er-do-well (nâr′dōōwel′)
    (a) idle, worthless person
    (b) a has-been
    (c) one who was aborted in mid-career
    (d) person worthy of recognition

3. to temporize (tem′pəriz′)
    (a) to lure or entice
    (b) to live in a temple
    (c) to delay making a decision to gain time
    (d) to prepare a Japanese dish of deep-fried seafood or vegetables

4. preternatural (prē′tərnachˌ′ərəl)
    (a) controlled by destiny
    (b) beyond what is regular in nature
    (c) characteristic of reptiles
    (d) mildly puzzled

5. palaver (pəlav′ər)
    (a) clash with a best friend
    (b) utter worthlessness
    (c) profuse and idle talk
    (d) covered or boxlike litter for one person carried by several men, formerly used in India and other Eastern countries

6. inquietude   (inkwī'it$\overline{oo}$d')
   (a) proper limits
   (b) interrogation
   (c) restlessness or uneasiness
   (d) loud noise

7. meerschaum   (mēr'shəm)
   (a) mineral occurring in white, claylike masses, used mainly for carvings
   (b) beard that curls in on itself
   (c) child who tends to be submissive
   (d) high amount of dark pigment in the legs

8. chimerical   (kimer'ikəl)
   (a) haunted
   (b) like a unicorn
   (c) like a queen of France
   (d) imaginary

9. aorta   (ā·ôr'tə)
   (a) another form of "either/or"
   (b) main trunk of the arterial system, conveying blood from the heart
   (c) point or rod on which a cello rests
   (d) drooping eyelid

10. farblondget   (fərblon'jət)
    (a) kept in the icebox
    (b) referring to a Muslim or Hindu religious ascetic or mendicant monk commonly considered a wonder worker
    (c) offering a high rate of interest
    (d) lost, mixed-up, wandering about without any idea where you are

___

Correct answers: 1 (b), 2 (a), 3 (c), 4 (b), 5 (c), 6 (c), 7 (a), 8 (d), 9 (b), 10 (d)

Your score:_____
(10–9 correct: superb; 8–6 correct: good; 5–4 correct: fair)

# What Our Presidents Didn't Know

Which President—while he was in office—did not know this expression because it was coined or came into usage during the *next* administration? (See the example on page 42.)

1. tractor _____

2. stereoscope _____

3. Muzak _____

4. maverick _____

5. cement _____

6. the big lie _____

7. to chisel (to cheat) _____

8. comedown (in status) _____

9. barnstorming _____

10. white-collar workers _____

_____

Correct answers: 1. James Monroe, 1817–25; 2. Andrew Jackson, 1829–37; 3. Herbert Hoover, 1929–33; 4. Abraham Lincoln, 1861–65; 5. James Madison, 1809–17; 6. Franklin D. Roosevelt, 1933–45; 7. John Quincy Adams, 1825–29; 8. Andrew Jackson, 1829–37; 9. Thomas Jefferson, 1801–09; 10. Calvin Coolidge, 1923–29

Your score: _____
(10–8 correct: superb; 7–4 correct: good; 3–2 correct: fair)

# Vocabulary Test No. 27

Which word or phrase is nearest in meaning to each of the
following headwords?

1. **taxonomy** (takson'əmē)
   - (a) the science dealing with the classification of plants
     and animals
   - (b) government department responsible for revenue col-
     lecting
   - (c) horsepower
   - (d) public vehicles (collectively)

2. **symmetry** (sim'itrē)
   - (a) meeting at which several speakers discuss a topic
     before an audience
   - (b) sign or indication of something
   - (c) representation of an object or an idea in chemistry
   - (d) correspondence in size and arrangement of parts on
     opposite sides

3. **perturbation** (pûr'tərbā'shen)
   - (a) coupled Ferris wheels
   - (b) mental disquiet or agitation
   - (c) noise unique to city life
   - (d) success neurosis

4. **precursor** (prikûr'sər)
   - (a) extremely abusive individual
   - (b) person or thing that precedes
   - (c) member of a religious order
   - (d) connection between or among things

5. **inchoate** (inkō'it)
   - (a) not organized or orderly
   - (b) weak-kneed

(c) in need
(d) having the tendency of keeping things secret

6. **incipient** (insipē·ənt)
   (a) roundabout or not direct
   (b) beginning to exist or appear
   (c) incapable of being comprehended
   (d) very good (informal)

7. **pedigree** (ped'əgrē')
   (a) perfect feet
   (b) case or object of dislike
   (c) examination of a body after death, as for determination of the cause of death
   (d) ancestral line

8. **menagerie** (mənaj'ərē)
   (a) a collection of wild or strange animals, esp. for exhibition
   (b) sharp and paroxysmal pain along a nerve
   (c) society or club
   (d) exhibition made of glass

9. **catholicity** (kath̲'əlis'itē)
   (a) noiselessness
   (b) universality or broad-mindedness
   (c) feline nature
   (d) extreme caution

10. **idiosyncrasy** (id'ē-əsing'krəsē)
    (a) asylum for the retarded and learning-disabled
    (b) religious worship of idols
    (c) habit or mannerism that is peculiar to an individual
    (d) collection of short poems on pastoral or rural life

---

Correct answers: 1 (a), 2 (d), 3 (b), 4 (b), 5 (a), 6 (b), 7 (d), 8 (a), 9 (b), 10 (c)

Your score:_____
(10–9 correct: superb; 8–6 correct: good; 5–4 correct: fair)

# Word Roots, Test I

Each of the following ten words stems from one of the three sources shown. Mark the correct answer.

1. bowel
   (a) from Latin *botulus*, "sausage"
   (b) from Thomas *Bowdler* (1754–1825), the English expurgator
   (c) from Old English *bolla*, "bowl"

2. gonad
   (a) from Greek *gonos*, "offspring"
   (b) extension of *gad*, a euphemistic interjection for *God*
   (c) from Italian *dondolare*, "to rock, to swing"

3. to constipate
   (a) from Latin *constans*, "constant"
   (b) from Latin *consors*, "sharing"
   (c) from Latin *constipare*, "to press together"

4. atrophy
   (a) from Latin *atrox*, "atrocious"
   (b) from Greek *atomos*, "not divisible"
   (c) from Greek *atrophos*, "not fed"

5. influenza
   (a) from Late Latin *influxus*, "astral influence"
   (b) from Medieval Latin *influentia*, "astral emanation"
   (c) from Latin *inflammare*, "to set on fire"

6. typhus
   (a) from Greek *tympanon*, "kettledrum"
   (b) from Greek *typhos*, "smoke, mist"
   (c) from Medieval Latin *tyrannia*, "tyranny"

7. cemetery
   (a) from Latin *caerimonia*, "ceremony"
   (b) from Latin *censor*, "assessor"
   (c) from Greek *koimeterion*, "sleeping place"

8. hearse
   (a) from Old English *heorte*, "heart"
   (b) from Old English *hoelan*, "heal"
   (c) from Medieval French *herce*, "candle frame"

9. autopsy
   (a) from Greek *automatos*, "self-moving"
   (b) from Greek *autarkeia*, "self-sufficiency"
   (c) from Greek *autopsia*, "seeing for oneself"

10. bacteria
    (a) from Greek *bakterion*, "little stick"
    (b) from Medieval English *badde*, "worthless"
    (c) from Old English *boeddel*, "effeminate person"

---

Correct answers: 1 (a), 2 (a), 3 (c), 4 (c), 5 (b), 6 (b), 7 (c), 8 (c), 9 (c), 10 (a)

Your score: _____
(10–9 correct: superb; 8–6 correct: good; 5–4 correct: fair)

148

# Yankee, Come Home!

## by Edward Gates

It seems most likely—and this origin is also favored by the *Oxford English Dictionary*—that the word *Yankee* entered the English language as a borrowing from the Dutch among British troops in Colonial New England. Its development illustrates several processes of change: shortening of form and extension, melioration, and degradation of meaning.

It originated in a mocking verse composed by a British army surgeon, a Dr. Shackburgh, who was quartered among the Dutch colonists along the Hudson River at the time the colonial troops were mustering for the French and Indian War in 1754:

> Yankee Doodle went to town,
> Riding on a pony.
> He stuck a feather in his hat
> And called it macaroni.

*Yankee* is probably a rendering of the Dutch *Janke* (Johnny), and *doodle* may also have been a Dutch word but had already been borrowed into English in the sense "a foolish fellow." Evidently, the British soldiers found the makeshift uniforms of some of the colonials amusing.

Set to a familiar folk tune (also heard with the words "Lucy Locket lost her pocket"), the verse was used by the British troops to poke fun at the colonists of New England, and the name "Yankee Doodle," shortened to *Yankee*, became a derisive epithet. It is said that the British marching to Lexington and Concord on April 19, 1775, sang this song. They were soundly defeated, and during their disorderly flight back to Boston the colonists mockingly asked them what they now thought of the *Yankees*. From then on, the colonists began to use the term of themselves with pride—a change of value that students of language call "melioration."

During the Civil War, Southerners called the Northern

troops *Yankees* with a strongly negative connotation. Again, the term was broadened to apply in Southern use to any Northerner.

During the First World War, American soldiers abroad were known as *Yankees*, in a positive sense, and this is seen in such songs as "Yankee Doodle Dandy" and "Over There" (which contains the line "The Yanks are coming," which is the shortened form).

After the Second World War, in some developing countries where Americans were unpopular, the term *Yankee* was given a negative connotation, seen in the slogan "Yankee, go home!" The word continues in current use largely in the positive meanings of a New Englander—especially one having the qualities of character traditionally associated with natives of that section—a Northerner and an American.

*Dr. Gates is Professor of English at Indiana State University.*

# Chapter X

## Vocabulary Test No. 28

Which word or phrase is nearest in meaning to each of the following headwords in the scientific vocabulary of the protean Isaac Asimov?

1. glucose  (glōō´kōs)
   - (a) sticky substance that holds together billions of cells
   - (b) "linchpin" in the construction of an Eskimo's home
   - (c) sum of the process that maintains, then destroys metabolism
   - (d) white sugar occurring in many fruits and having a sweetness about one half that of ordinary sugar

2. parabola  (pərab´ələ)
   - (a) short story designed to convey a truth or moral lesson about alchemists
   - (b) plane curve formed by the intersection of a cone and a plane parallel to one of its sides
   - (c) example serving as a model
   - (d) statement seemingly self-contradictory, but in reality expressing a possible truth

3. catalysis  (kətal´isis)
   - (a) universal code of life
   - (b) state of mind brought on by repeated blows to the head

151

(c) chemical change by the addition of a substance that itself remains unchanged

(d) a tree of the U.S., having large leaves and bell-shaped white flowers

4. **occult** (əkult')
   (a) blindly following one's mentor
   (b) beyond the range of ordinary knowledge
   (c) feeding on human flesh
   (d) having a soft, oval body (as a sea mollusk)

5. **amphibious** (amfib'e·əs)
   (a) living both on land and in water
   (b) not entirely truthful about one's scientific research
   (c) pertaining to a two-winged airplane
   (d) having a three-pronged electrical socket

6. **parsec** (pär'sek')
   (a) sudden outburst of emotion
   (b) three parallel lines emitted by a quasar
   (c) astronomical tool used by early telescope users to measure the distance from the Earth to canals on Mars
   (d) unit of distance equal to that required to cause a heliocentric parallax of one second of an arc

7. **vitriol** (vi'trē·əl)
   (a) decisive rebuke
   (b) something severely caustic, as criticism
   (c) unctuousness
   (d) disease affecting only Eastern European Jews

8. **Chiroptera** (kīrɒp'tərə)
   (a) the order comprising the bats
   (b) foot fungus
   (c) the order comprising the butterflies
   (d) Pharaoh's architectual staff responsible for the pyramids

9. **fossil** (fos'əl)
   (a) animal or plant that cannot be converted to mineral
   (b) ledge on which the window rests

(c) remains or trace of an animal or plant of a former geological age

(d) the study of very old trees

10. cumulus (kyōō'myələs)
   (a) clouds with dense elements in the form of puffs
   (b) animal organism
   (c) dictator's desire to be foremost in scientific effort and success
   (d) state of bewilderment in an individual suddenly exposed to a cultural environment radically different from his own

---

Correct answers: 1 (d), 2 (b), 3 (c), 4 (b), 5 (a), 6 (d), 7 (b), 8 (a), 9 (c), 10 (a)

Your score: _____
(10–9 correct: superb; 8–6 correct: good; 5–4 correct: fair)

153

# Eponyms

The items at the left refer to proper names; the items at the right define words or phrases that are derived from these proper names. Match them.

Example:
a fishmarket in London _____ coarsely or vulgarly abusive language

The answer is "billingsgate" (Billingsgate).

1. a city in Morocco _____

2. a town in Pennsylvania _____

3. a German state _____

4. a town in Belgium _____

5. a valley in West Germany _____

6. a city in East Germany _____

7. an American horticulturist _____

8. a fictitious country inhabited by tiny people _____

9. a U.S. minister to Mexico _____

10. a son of Noah _____

(a) a red cap, shaped like a truncated cone, with a black tassel, worn esp. by men in the Near East

(b) extremely small; petty or trivial

(c) a type of fine porcelain

(d) a broad-wheeled covered wagon, used esp. in North America during the early westward migration

(e) a breed of black-and-white dairy cattle yielding large quantities of low-fat milk

(f) a member of any of various ancient and modern peoples including the Hebrews and Arabs

(g) a large, cylindrical canvas bag for carrying personal effects

(h) a plant native to tropical America, with tiny flowers surrounded by large, bright-red leaves

(i) a member of an extinct race of prehistoric people who lived in caves; rugged or uncouth

(j) the large, dark-red, acid fruit of a blackberrylike plant

---

Correct answers: 1 (a) fez (Fez), 2 (d) Conestoga wagon (Conestoga), 3 (e) Holstein, 4 (g) duffel bag (Duffel), 5 (i) Neanderthal, 6 (c) Dresden china (Dresden), 7 (j) loganberry (J. H. Logan, 1841–1928), 8 (b) Lilliputian (Lilliput), 9 (h) poinsettia (J. R. Poinsett, 1779–1851), 10 (f) Semite (Shem)

Your score: _____
(10–9 correct: superb; 8–6 correct: good; 5–4 correct: fair)

# Vocabulary Test No. 29

Which word or phrase is nearest in meaning to each of the following headwords?

1. proclivity (prōkliv′itē)
   (a) winning gesture
   (b) strong habitual inclination or tendency
   (c) test or trial
   (d) habit of delaying action till another day or time

2. scruple (skroo′pəl)
   (a) untidy arrangement
   (b) spray driven by the wind
   (c) artist who works in sculpture
   (d) ethical consideration as a restraining force

3. obstinate (ob′stənit)
   (a) fearful
   (b) stubborn and unyielding
   (c) dulling the mind
   (d) outmoded

4. aversion (əvur′zhən)
   (a) denial
   (b) malicious or damaging statement
   (c) strong dislike
   (d) crooked or selfish deed

5. dogmatic (dôgmat′ik)
   (a) asserting opinions in an arrogant manner
   (b) rough in temper or manner
   (c) insistent
   (d) imperious

6. **to tergiversate** (tûr′jivərsāt′)
   (a) to evolve
   (b) to be capable of being held, maintained, or defended
   (c) to change one's attitude repeatedly
   (d) to make a friendly gesture, usually with open palms

7. **caprice** (kəprēs′)
   (a) touchstone of a career
   (b) upsetting decision
   (c) sudden, unpredictable change
   (d) judicial opinion

8. **indefatigable** (in′difat′əgəbəl)
   (a) not harmonious in character
   (b) incapable of being tired out
   (c) without logical connection
   (d) not clearly defined or determined

9. **vagary** (vəgâr′ē)
   (a) unsuccessful or futile attempt
   (b) unexpected excretion
   (c) masturbation
   (d) unpredictable or erratic action

10. **incorrigible** (inkôr′ijəbəl)
    (a) bad beyond reform
    (b) receptive to encouragement
    (c) plentifully abundant
    (d) capable of suicide

---

Correct answers: 1 (b), 2 (d), 3 (b), 4 (c), 5 (a), 6 (c), 7 (c), 8 (b), 9 (d), 10 (a)

Your score:_____
(10–9 correct: superb; 8–6 correct: good; 5–4 correct: fair)

********************************************************************

# Fill In the Blanks

Example:
marked by a lofty or grandiose style:
__ a g n __ __ o __ u __ __ t

The answer is "magniloquent."

1. slow-witted person: n __ __ __ __ u __ l

2. (a girl) suitable for marriage, esp. in regard to age or physical development: __ u __ i l e

3. round in shape; plump or fat: r __ t __ n __

4. mere repetition of memorized words or sounds without thought for meaning: __ __ t __

5. to set forth publicly; to put into operation (a law, etc.) by formal proclamation: p __ o m __ l __ __ t __

6. a large, loose cloak, usually hooded, worn with a small mask in masquerade: __ __ m i __ __

7. a departure from one's religion or cause: __ p __ s __ __ __ y

8. a moral or ethical consideration that acts as a restraining force; a unit of apothecaries' weight equal to twenty grains: s __ __ u p __ e

9. to kiss: o __ __ __ __ a t e

10. presumptuously conceited or proud; immoderate or excessive: __ __ __ __ __ e e n __ __ __

---

Correct answers: 1. numskull 2. nubile 3. rotund 4. rote 5. promulgate 6. domino 7. apostasy 8. scruple 9. osculate 10. overweening

Your score: _____
(10–9 correct: superb; 8–6 correct: good; 5–4 correct: fair)

# Vocabulary Test No. 30

Which word or phrase is nearest in meaning to each of the
following headwords?

1. consanguineous   (kon'sang·gwin'ē·əs)
   (a) known to oneself
   (b) having the same ancestry
   (c) self-important or conceited
   (d) not subject to decay

2. synonym   (sin'ənim)
   (a) mark of sophistication
   (b) word having nearly the same meaning as another
   (c) intuitive conjecture
   (d) the act of surprising

3. monotonous   (mənot'˘nəs)
   (a) not here
   (b) tiresomely uniform
   (c) tedious
   (d) neither here nor there

4. mimicry   (mim'ikrē)
   (a) imitation in action or appearance
   (b) slender tower attached to a mosque
   (c) utterance of the unspoken words of another
   (d) mental vision or imagination

5. simulacrum   (sim'yəlā'krəm)
   (a) the buying or selling of benefices
   (b) silly, self-conscious smile
   (c) railroad boxcar
   (d) unreal or superficial semblance

6. **multifarious** (mul'təfâr'ē·əs)
   (a) Januslike
   (b) having wide variety or great diversity
   (c) lacking in mental acuteness
   (d) orgiastic

7. **paucity** (pô'sitē)
   (a) franchise
   (b) smallness of number or amount
   (c) lapse in memory
   (d) scene of an accident

8. **prodigious** (prədij'əs)
   (a) insouciant
   (b) in accord with (someone or something)
   (c) extraordinary in size or amount
   (d) troubled by suspicions of rivalry or unfaithfulness

9. **crass** (kras)
   (a) without refinement or sensitivity
   (b) quarrelsome, grouchy, irritable
   (c) growing in fresh water
   (d) pious and platitudinous

10. **anabasis** (ənab'əsis)
    (a) medieval association of merchants or tradesmen
    (b) son-in-law
    (c) defense of cherished beliefs or traditional institutions
    (d) military expedition

---

Correct answers: 1 (b), 2 (b), 3 (b), 4 (a), 5 (d), 6 (b), 7 (b), 8 (c), 9 (a), 10 (d)

Your score: _____
(10–9 correct: superb; 8–6 correct: good; 5–4 correct: fair)

# Word Roots, Test J

Each of the following ten words stems from one of the three sources shown. Mark the correct answer.

1. libertine
   (a) from Latin *libido*, "desire"
   (b) from Latin *libertinus*, "freedman"
   (c) from *Liberia*, the ancient Italian goddess of fertility

2. pundit
   (a) from Middle English *punchen*, "punch"
   (b) from Spanish *punta*, "point"
   (c) from Hindi *pandit*, "scholar"

3. cynic
   (a) from Greek *kyklos*, "circle"
   (b) from Greek *kynikos*, "doglike"
   (c) from Russian *tsar*, "emperor"

4. amateur
   (a) from Old English *amasian*, "to confuse"
   (b) from Latin *manus*, "hand"
   (c) from Latin *amator*, "lover"

5. marvel
   (a) from Spanish *mascara*, "mask"
   (b) from Latin *martialis*, "of Mars"
   (c) from Latin *mirabilia*, "wonderful things"

6. interlocutor
   (a) from Latin *inter-*, "between," plus Dutch *lopen*, "to run" (one who intrudes into the affairs of others)
   (b) from Latin *intermedius*, "intermediate"
   (c) from Latin *interloqui*, "to speak between"

7. person
   (a) from Latin *persona*, "mask"
   (b) from Latin *perspicax*, "sharp-sighted"
   (c) from Latin *perspirare*, "to breathe through"

8. scion
   (a) from Old French *cion*, "shoot, twig"
   (b) from Arabic *cifr*, "zero"
   (c) from Latin *scintilla*, "spark"

9. dame
   (a) from Latin *domina*, "lady"
   (b) from Latin *damnare*, "to condemn"
   (c) from Latin *damnum*, "loss"

10. infant
    (a) from Latin *infamia*, "ill fame"
    (b) from Latin *infantis*, "not speaking"
    (c) from Latin *infra*, "below"

---

Correct answers: 1 (b), 2 (c), 3 (b), 4 (c), 5 (c), 6 (c), 7 (a), 8 (a), 9 (a), 10 (b)

Your score:_____
(10–9 correct: superb; 8–6 correct: good; 5–4 correct: fair)

# Something New under the Sun

### by B. H. Smeaton

In the latter Forties, when I worked in Saudi Arabia for Aramco, I asked a houseboy to throw out some flowers that I had in a vase (they had dried up, for lack of water). He was dusting and wanted the odd job. "They're dead," I explained (in Arabic: *Hum mayyitīn* ...). He thought that was uproariously funny, and he even told a couple of the other houseboys (*boyyah*) about it. So I asked him what he'd say, if not "dead flowers"? (Naturally, only a crazy Westerner would put flowers in a vase anyway.) "You'd say they were dry, not dead," he informed me ( ...*hum yābisīn* ...). Later, I realized that Islam doesn't have "animal, vegetable, and mineral kingdoms"; there is an opposition between live creatures and things, and things embrace non-animal life, too: vegetable and mineral are one (contrast our threefold breakdown). For that matter, orthodox Islam bans pictures of animals (consider the Alhambra). Note also the Saudi Arabian postage stamps of that day, which showed only palm trees—and a tree, to Sunni Moslems, is no more alive than a rock.

*Dr. Smeaton is Professor of Linguistics at the University of Calgary, Canada.*

# Chapter XI

## Vocabulary Test No. 31

Which word or phrase is nearest in meaning to each of the following headwords from the informal vocabulary known as slang?

1. peeties
   (a) mini-agates
   (b) coming attractions (movies)
   (c) loaded dice
   (d) balls of coal chips

2. clown wagon
   (a) bank teller's station
   (b) freight train's caboose
   (c) police van
   (d) orbiting space station

3. steam fiddle
   (a) fire-breathing magician, usually an amateur
   (b) dragon
   (c) open manhole
   (d) calliope

4. old Sol
   (a) very old street fiddler
   (b) the Sun
   (c) delicatessen owner
   (d) Biblical prophet (diminutive)

5. **one-way guy**
   - (a) honest, fair, or sincere man
   - (b) heterosexual man
   - (c) mother's boy
   - (d) papa's boy

6. **barnyard golf**
   - (a) pig in heat
   - (b) game of pitching horseshoes
   - (c) chopping off a chicken's head
   - (d) group sex

7. **give me five**
   - (a) let's shake (or slap) hands
   - (b) lend me money (usually five figures)
   - (c) help me to cheat (on a public-service examination)
   - (d) let's watch a five-minute home video porn tape

8. **forty-four**
   - (a) prostitute
   - (b) buck private in a peacetime army
   - (c) border between the U.S. and Canada
   - (d) the retaking of an IQ examination

9. **chucklehead**
   - (a) steeplechase
   - (b) laughing gas
   - (c) animated squirrel
   - (d) stupid person

10. **Jonah**
   - (a) early edition of a major metropolitan daily
   - (b) large whale
   - (c) a hipster, a rock, a cat
   - (d) grand-slam home run

---

Correct answers: 1 (c), 2 (b), 3 (d), 4 (b), 5 (a), 6 (b), 7 (a), 8 (a), 9 (d), 10 (c)

Your score:_____
(10–9 correct: superb; 8–6 correct: good; 5–4 correct: fair)

# What We Do to Our Children

Match the numbers with the letters.

THE NAME

1. Amos _____
2. Barbara _____
3. Blaze, Blasius _____
4. Calvin _____
5. Cameron _____
6. Campbell _____
7. Cecilia, Cecil _____
8. Claudia, Claude _____
9. Dolores, Lola, Lolita _____
10. Doreen _____
11. Gladys _____
12. Gretta _____
13. Hagar _____
14. Humbert _____
15. Humphrey _____
16. Lona _____
17. Mary, Mara, Miriam _____
18. Mona _____
19. Natica _____
20. Paul, Pablo, Paula _____
21. Priscilla _____
22. Rachel, Raquel, Rae _____
23. Rebecca _____
24. Ulysses _____
25. Ursula _____
26. Vaughn _____

MEANT OR MEANS

(a) the bald one (Late Latin)

(b) the sullen one (Irish Gaelic)

(c) the bitter one, bitterness (Hebrew)

(d) the buttock (Italian)

(e) the small one (Latin)

(f) the small one (Old Welsh)

(g) a burden (Hebrew)

(h) the mean, petty, stingy one (Italian—though the name is meant to come from German)

(i) a female monkey (Spanish—though the

167

name has a variety of sources)

(j) a foreigner, the uncivilized one (literally, the stammering one— Greek)

(k) the stammerer (Latin)

(l) sorrows, the suffering one (Spanish)

(m) the one who is somewhat old (Latin)

(n) the one with the crooked nose (Scotch Gaelic)

(o) the lonely one (Middle English)

(p) the one with the crooked mouth (Scotch Gaelic)

(q) the bound one (Hebrew)

(r) a female sheep (Hebrew)

(s) the hater (Greek)

(t) the blind or dim-sighted one (Latin)

(u) the forsaken one (Hebrew)

(v) a little female bear (Latin)

(w) the brilliant hun (Old Germanic)

(x) the peaceful hun (Old Germanic)

(y) the lame or limping one (Latin)

(z) the lame or limping one (Old Welsh)

---

Correct answers: 1 (g), 2 (j), 3 (k), 4 (a), 5 (n), 6 (p), 7 (t), 8 (y), 9 (l), 10 (b), 11 (z), 12 (h), 13 (u), 14 (w), 15 (x), 16 (o), 17 (c), 18 (i), 19 (d), 20 (e), 21 (m), 22 (r), 23 (q), 24 (s), 25 (v), 26 (f)

Your score:_____
(26–22 correct: superb; 21–15 correct: good; 14–10 correct: fair)

# Vocabulary Test No. 32

Which word or phrase is nearest in meaning to each of the following headwords, which are used by Carl Sagan (*Cosmos, The Cosmic Connection, Other Worlds*)

1. indigenous   (indij'ənəs)
   (a)  originating in a particular region
   (b)  beneath one's dignity
   (c)  denoting a frequency below the range of human hearing
   (d)  extraterrestrial

2. quasar   (kwā'sär)
   (a)  sixteen-pointed star in the Milky Way
   (b)  granular rock consisting essentially of quartz in interlocking grains
   (c)  suppression of a rebellion
   (d)  distant, powerful celestial source of radio energy

3. exobiology   (ek'sōbī·ol'əjē)
   (a)  the study of life beyond the Earth's atmosphere
   (b)  the study of sea plants
   (c)  the study of biological claims
   (d)  the study of extinct forms of life

4. sycophant   (sik'əfənt)
   (a)  imagination or fancy
   (b)  self-seeking, servile flatterer
   (c)  organized group of gangsters
   (d)  the combining of separate parts or elements to form a whole

5. molecule   (mol'əkyōōl')
   (a)  flat sheet of microfilm, typically 4 × 6 inches
   (b)  tooth in prehistoric man having a broad biting surface

     (c)  smallest physical unit of an element or compound that can exist with separate identity
     (d)  tail-less ferret

6. **vesicular** (vəsik'yələr)
     (a)  containing mustard gas
     (b)  pertaining to a small sac or cyst
     (c)  ceremonial
     (d)  imperfectly developed

7. **googol** (gōō'gol)
     (a)  first word of a star child
     (b)  peanut
     (c)  the number 1 followed by one hundred zeros
     (d)  glutton

8. **albedo** (albē'dō)
     (a)  a ratio of light reflection and reception
     (b)  solar wing of a space satellite
     (c)  large bronze disk that produces a vibrant, hollow tone when struck
     (d)  purulent inflammation of the urethra

9. **inverse** (invûrs')
     (a)  not having made a will
     (b)  opposite in position or tendency
     (c)  discovered last
     (d)  characterized by warm friendship

10. **voluble** (vol'yəbəl)
     (a)  fluent in speech, or talkative
     (b)  willing or choosing
     (c)  twisted
     (d)  pertaining to the DNA structure

---

Correct answers: 1 (a), 2 (d), 3 (a), 4 (b), 5 (c), 6 (b), 7 (c), 8 (a), 9 (b), 10 (a)

Your score:_____
(10–9 correct: superb; 8–6 correct: good; 5–4 correct: fair)

# There *Is* a Word for It

Example:
a person who is lord over another or over other lords:
o_____

The answer is "overlord."

1. a dining hall, esp. in a cloister: r_____

2. an expression of the face marked by a turning up of the corners of the mouth, usually indicating pleasure or amusement: s_____

3. a whip formerly used in Russia for flogging criminals: k_____

4. a trace or visible evidence of something that is no longer present or in existence: v_____

5. the side of a hog salted and cured:
f_____

6. to force (a person) to join the crew of a ship, esp. by using drugs or liquor: s_____

7. a writer of low-quality verse: p_____

8. a Hawaiian dish made of taro root:
p_____

9. exceedingly fastidious: p_____

10. expectorated matter, as saliva or spittle mixed with mucus: s_____

**Correct answers:** 1. refrectory 2. smile 3. knout 4. vestige 5. flitch 6. shanghai 7. poetaster 8. poi 9. persnickety 10. sputum

**Your score:** _____
(10–9 correct: superb; 8–6 correct: good; 5–4 correct: fair)

# Vocabulary Test No. 33

Which word or phrase is nearest in meaning to each of the following headwords?

1. to circumvent (sûr'kəmvent')
   - (a) to outwit or get the better of (someone or a situation)
   - (b) to travel around the globe
   - (c) to take blood
   - (d) to remove the prepuce, esp. as a religious rite

2. to discomfit (diskum'fit)
   - (a) to confuse and deject
   - (b) to cause to vanish
   - (c) to irritate
   - (d) to frolic

3. titubation (tich'ŏŏbā'shən)
   - (a) disturbance of body balance
   - (b) loud, sudden thunderclap (literally out of the blue)
   - (c) exhaustion
   - (d) slight coloration

4. halcyon (hal'sē·ən)
   - (a) lucky
   - (b) pertaining to a whirlpool
   - (c) peaceful and calm
   - (d) sunny

5. providential (prov'iden'shəl)
   - (a) of a subtle nature
   - (b) seeming to come from divine intervention
   - (c) coming from a work of art
   - (d) careful in planning for the future

173

6. to consummate   (kon'səmāt')
   (a) to eat a dinner, from soup to nuts
   (b) to resemble a blood relative
   (c) to bring to fulfillment
   (d) to be initiated

7. felicitous   (filis'itəs)
   (a) overwhelming
   (b) gratuitous
   (c) endearing
   (d) well-suited for the occasion

8. palmy   (pä'mē)
   (a) glorious or prosperous
   (b) of the size of a man's hand
   (c) despicably small
   (d) throbbing

9. to quell   (kwel)
   (a) to shake and rattle
   (b) to suppress or crush
   (c) to ooze
   (d) to spring up or out

10. swimmingly   (swim'iṅglē)
   (a) openly
   (b) secretly
   (c) without difficulty
   (d) against mild resistance

---

Correct answers: 1 (a), 2 (a), 3 (a), 4 (c), 5 (b), 6 (c), 7 (d),
8 (a), 9 (b), 10 (c)

Your score:_____
(10–9 correct: superb; 8–6 correct: good; 5–4 correct: fair)

174

# Word Roots, Test K

Each of the following ten words stems from one of the three sources shown. Mark the correct answer.

1. candidate
   - (a) from Medieval Latin *cancellare*, "to cross out"
   - (b) from Latin *candela*, "candle"
   - (c) from Latin *candidatus*, "white-robed"

2. tycoon
   - (a) from Maori *tiki* (the mythological first man on Earth)
   - (b) from *Tyche*, the Greek goddess of fortune
   - (c) from Japanese *taikun*, "great prince"

3. proletariat
   - (a) from Latin *prolixus*, "extended"
   - (b) from Latin *promiscuus*, "mixed up"
   - (c) from Latin *proletarius*, "citizen whose (sole) contribution consists in making children" (that is, of the lowest class)

4. police
   - (a) from Greek *politeia*, "government"
   - (b) from Middle English *pollax*, "head ax"
   - (c) from Greek *polemos*, "war"

5. campaign
   - (a) from *Chamyne*, an alternative name of the Greek goddess Demeter, protectress of the social order
   - (b) from Italian *campana*, "bell"
   - (c) from French *campagne*, "country"

6. franchise
   - (a) from Old English *framian*, "to be helpful"
   - (b) from Old French *franc*, "free"
   - (c) from Latin *frater*, "brother"

7. tong
   (a) from Latin *tonsura*, "a shearing"
   (b) from Indi *tamtam*, "tom-tom"
   (c) from Chinese *t'ang*, "meeting hall"

8. kremlin
   (a) from Latin *crimen*, "crime"
   (b) from Old English *cringan*, "to yield"
   (c) from Russian *kreml'*, "fortress"

9. cartel
   (a) from French *carte blanche*, "blank card"
   (b) from Middle English *carole*, "ring"
   (c) from Old Italian *cartello*, "poster"

10. ballot
   (a) from Late Latin *ballare*, "to dance"
   (b) from Latin *balsamum*, "balsam"
   (c) from Italian *ballotta*, "little ball"

---

Correct answers: 1 (c), 2 (c), 3 (c), 4 (a), 5 (c), 6 (b), 7 (c), 8 (c), 9 (c), 10 (c)

Your score: _____
(10–9 correct: superb; 8–6 correct: good; 5–4 correct: fair)

# From the Boondocks

### by Willis Barnstone

*Hunky-dory*: I was told it meant "main street" in Japanese. In a Japanese city, the main street leads down to the harbor, so when American sailors, drunk and lost, had to find their way back to ship, the one word that would save them was *hunky-dory*. So it came to mean everything is now fine, okay. When I was in Japan, I asked for *hunky-dory*, and there I found myself on the main street of a coastal city, on the way to the port.

*Hubba hubba*: A Second World War word that soldiers and sailors used to mean okay, everything's fine. I never understood why until I studied Chinese at Middlebury College language school and constantly heard all summer *hau-bu-hau*, meaning okay, fine, or "Is it okay?"—depending on use. It means literally "good-not-good?"

*Boondocks*: I live in the *boondocks*. So I discovered two decades ago when I moved to Indiana. So everyone identified my new area, that is, those outsiders I reached by long distance. But Indiana is at most hilly, and *boondocks* comes from a Tagalog word meaning mountain. But the more general meaning is wilderness or backwoods or jungle. In a Chinese restaurant in Madrid I asked the Filipino waitress how to say mountain in Tagalog. She immediately replied *bundok*, and so my friends believed my story of the origin of the word.

*Chifa*: In Peru one night, we ate in a Chinese restaurant called a *chifa*. I recognized this as the Chinese word for "eating rice," *ch'ih fàn*. The Chinese word for restaurant is *fàn-kuăn* (pronounced *"fanguan"*). It reminded me of an afternoon in central China with some American and English friends who were appalled by a parrot who could speak Chinese when they

177

couldn't utter a word. Of course, the parrot was saying *wo yau ch'ih fàn*, "I want to eat rice," meaning "I want something to eat."

*Dr. Barnstone is Professor of Comparative Literature at Indiana University.*

# Chapter XII

## Vocabulary Test No. 34

Which word or phrase is nearest in meaning to each of the following headwords, which are used in discussing Egyptology?

1. phonetics (fənet'iks)
   (a) incorrect reading of stone writing
   (b) the study of Alexandrian work on the telephone in the century before Bell patented his invention
   (c) archival documents on early languages
   (d) the study of speech processes

2. papyrus (pəpī'rəs)
   (a) ancient paperlike material made from a reedlike plant
   (b) writing material of the Babylonians
   (c) symbol for excellence in the ancient world
   (d) powder that relieves pain

3. obelisk (ob'əlisk)
   (a) astronomical marker
   (b) four-sided tapered shaft of stone
   (c) construction in the African deserts to indicate underground water supplies
   (d) stone carvings that related the news of the day in the Fertile Crescent

179

4. philology   (filol'əjē)
   (a) the love of twin brothers in Homeric adventures
   (b) the study of written texts, esp. of literary works
   (c) the collection and study of the earliest postage stamps
   (d) federation of lawyers in the Golden Age of Greece skilled in matters involving fine points and technicalities

5. pagan   (pā'gən)
   (a) irreligious person
   (b) the very first event in the very first Olympiad
   (c) bird that is displayed repeatedly in hieroglyphic writings
   (d) a god to whom South Pacific peoples donated human sacrifices

6. deism   (dē'izəm)
   (a) condensation of moisture from the air
   (b) payment to pyramid builders engaged on a day-to-day basis
   (c) belief in the existence of God on the evidence of reason only
   (d) worship of the printed word

7. cuneiform   (kyo͞onē'əfôrm')
   (a) pertaining to hair designs that conveyed feelings between men and women in Jordan
   (b) wedge-shaped
   (c) carved in sand
   (d) pertaining to the Sumerian god of love, usually represented as a winged, naked infant boy with a bow and arrows

8. Coptic   (kop'tik)
   (a) extinct language of Egypt that developed from ancient Egyptian
   (b) vehicle known today as the spaceship of Ezekiel
   (c) Egyptian version of the Torah
   (d) bark on which the infant Moses was placed by his mother

9. cartouche   (kärtoōsh')
   (a) cliché
   (b) clever point made by a sage
   (c) oblong figure, as on ancient Egyptian monuments, enclosing the name of a sovereign
   (d) key to deciphering the Rosetta Stone

10. demotic   (dimot'ik)
    (a) studying the demons in earliest writings
    (b) in the manner of oarsmen on a Nile barge
    (c) mysterious
    (d) pertaining to the common people

---

Correct answers: 1 (d), 2 (a), 3 (b), 4 (b), 5 (a), 6 (c), 7 (b), 8 (a), 9 (c), 10 (d)

Your score: _____
(10–9 correct: superb; 8–6 correct: good; 5–4 correct: fair)

# Scramblings

Each phrase defines the word that follows it in scrambled form. Can you put the eggs back together again?

Example:
a small, round skullcap worn by Roman Catholic ecclesiastics:
ttccohezu _____

The answer is "zucchetto."

1. formal praise: uimmocen _____

2. a region on the border of hell or heaven for some souls, as those of unbaptized infants; a place or state of oblivion; a place midway between two extremes:
olbmi _____

3. working or acting merely for money or other reward; a professional soldier: crrmnyeae _____

4. wild lawlessness or uproar:
namepnmuiod _____

5. malicious and unjustifiable; without regard for what is right or humane: twnoan _____

6. holiness or piety of life; sacred or hallowed character:
citynsat _____

7. full of twists, turns, or bends; deceitfully indirect:
stourout _____

8. a player of the double bass: sssbtia _____

9. an incidental or passing remark or opinion:
roebit ticmud _____

10. viscid or sticky: ogsulutin _____

_____

Correct answers: 1. encomium 2. limbo 3. mercenary 4. pandemonium 5. wanton 6. sanctity 7. tortuous 8. bassist 9. obiter dictum 10. glutinous

Your score:_____
(10–9 correct: superb; 8–6 correct: good; 5–4 correct: fair)

# Vocabulary Test No. 35

Which word or phrase is nearest in meaning to each of the following headwords?

1. salubrious (səlōō′brē·əs)
    (a) easy to solve
    (b) favorable to health
    (c) alike in a general way but not exactly
    (d) having keen mental discernment and sound judgment

2. to debase (dibās′)
    (a) to step down
    (b) to prepare for surgery
    (c) to reduce in quality or value
    (d) to inspire

3. slattern (slat′ərn)
    (a) slovenly, untidy woman
    (b) window blinds
    (c) brutal, violent killing, esp. of many people
    (d) haphazard action

4. galore (gəlōr′)
    (a) star-spangled
    (b) in plentiful amounts
    (c) pertaining to the female owner of a bar cum restaurant
    (d) golden

5. to minister (min′istər)
    (a) to give care or aid
    (b) to insist on one's duties
    (c) to terminate a trial without conclusion because of some error in the proceedings
    (d) to preach

6. surfeit   (sûr′fit)
   (a) curl of a high wave
   (b) insurance for a new-born
   (c) excessive amount
   (d) Japanese form of wrestling, usually by men of great height and weight


7. copious   (kō′pē·əs)
   (a) sincerely remorseful
   (b) shedding great tears
   (c) bought for the honeymoon
   (d) plentifully abundant


8. paragon   (par′əgon′)
   (a) dying star
   (b) model of excellence
   (c) intuition
   (d) selection made up of elements from different sources


9. scavenger   (skav′injər)
   (a) seaman
   (b) murderer
   (c) person or animal that searches through refuse for usable articles
   (d) scion


10. to emend   (imend′)
   (a) to add to, as to a salary
   (b) to add another floor (to a building)
   (c) to edit (a text) by removing flaws
   (d) to act as a master of ceremonies

---

Correct answers: 1 (b), 2 (c), 3 (a), 4 (b), 5 (a), 6 (c), 7 (d), 8 (b), 9 (c), 10 (c)

Your score:_____
(10–9 correct: superb; 8–6 correct: good; 5–4 correct: fair)

# What Our Presidents Didn't Know

Which President—while he was in office—did not know this expression because it was coined or came into usage during the *next* administration? (See the example on page 42.)

1. pitcher's mound: _____

2. blockbuster: _____

3. gobbledygook: _____

4. toxic-shock syndrome: _____

5. beat generation: _____

6. robot: _____

7. dynamo: _____

8. hotdog: _____

9. UFO: _____

10. chop suey: _____

_____

Correct answers: 1. William Howard Taft, 1909–13; 2. Herbert Hoover, 1929–33; 3. Herbert Hoover, 1929–33; 4. Gerald Ford, 1974–77; 5. Harry S Truman, 1945–53; 6. Woodrow Wilson, 1913–21; 7. John Quincy Adams, 1825–29; 8. Grover Cleveland, 1893–97; 9. Harry S Truman, 1945–53; 10. Benjamin Harrison, 1889–93

Your score: _____
(10–8 correct: superb; 7–4 correct: good; 3–2 correct: fair)

# Vocabulary Test No. 36

Which word or phrase is nearest in meaning to each of the following headwords, which center on antagonisms in a variety of guises?

1. incursion (inkûr'zhən)
   (a) slash by sword across an arm
   (b) inquisition
   (c) encumbrance
   (d) hostile, usually sudden, invasion of a place

2. vexation (veksā'shən)
   (a) soothing ointment for forehead and throat to help lower the body's temperature
   (b) something that irritates and disturbs provokingly
   (c) long, bitter feud
   (d) movement in a seesaw fashion

3. onerous (on'ərəs)
   (a) annoyingly or unfairly burdensome
   (b) biting
   (c) imitating natural sounds
   (d) deserving of reprobation

4. succor (suk'ər)
   (a) timely aid in distress
   (b) juice
   (c) large mouth
   (d) pressure by gas

5. to thwart (thwôrt)
   (a) to strike forcibly
   (b) to move away, as from danger
   (c) to oppose successfully
   (d) to cut off a foe's nose

6. **demagogue**   (dem′əgôg′)
   (a) puppet governor
   (b) propaganda director
   (c) digression of ten years
   (d) person who tries to gain popularity by appealing to emotions and prejudices

7. **donnybrook**   (don′ēbrŏók′)
   (a) decimation
   (b) wild, noisy fight
   (c) conflict over water rights
   (d) military operation

8. **concord**   (kon′kôrd)
   (a) harmonious agreement in ideas or feelings
   (b) thin rubber sheath worn over the penis during intercourse to prevent conception or infection
   (c) an official position by the Roman Catholic Church
   (d) solid mass formed by coalescence or cohesion

9. **retribution**   (re′tri·byōō′shən)
   (a) acceptance by vendor of improperly produced goods
   (b) enjoyment based on false beliefs or hopes
   (c) rejection on moral grounds of a honor proferred
   (d) punishment given in return for some wrong

10. **polemic**   (pəlem′ik)
   (a) mechanical response, or uninterested routine
   (b) controversial argument, as against some opinion
   (c) two-headed hammer
   (d) lummox with authority

---

Correct answers: 1 (d), 2 (b), 3 (a), 4 (a), 5 (c), 6 (d), 7 (b), 8 (a), 9 (d), 10 (b)

Your score:_____
(10–9 correct: superb; 8–6 correct: good; 5–4 correct: fair)

# Word Roots, Test L

Each of the following ten words stems from one of the three sources shown. Mark the correct answer.

1. dipsomania
   (a) from Greek *dipsa*, "thirst"
   (b) from *Dionysus*, the Greek god of wine
   (c) from Greek *diphthera*, "skin"

2. hysteria
   (a) from Greek *hyssopos*, "hyssop" (a fragrant medicinal herb)
   (b) from Greek *hystera*, "womb"
   (c) from Latin *histrio*, "actor"

3. dexterity
   (a) from Latin *dexter*, "right hand"
   (b) from *Dexter*, a town in Missouri
   (c) from Old English *dysig*, "foolish"

4. ardor
   (a) from Latin *ardere*, "to burn"
   (b) from Latin *arduus*, "steep"
   (c) from Latin *arare*, "to plow"

5. ambition
   (a) from Latin *amplus*, "wide"
   (b) from Latin *ambitio*, "going about, in canvassing votes"
   (c) from Middle French *amener*, "to lead up"

6. illusion
   (a) from Latin *illustris*, "bright"
   (b) from Lenin's true name, Nikolai Vladimir *Ilyich* Ulyanov
   (c) from Latin *illusio*, "irony"

7. scruple
   (a) from Latin *scrupulus*, "small pebble"
   (b) from Norwegian *skudda*, "to push"
   (c) from *scrubby*

8. consternation
   (a) from Latin *constringere*, "to constrain"
   (b) from Latin *contestari*, "to call to witness"
   (c) from Latin *consternare*, "to terrify"

9. malice
   (a) from Latin *masculus*, "male"
   (b) from Latin *malitia*, "evil"
   (c) from Latin *malleare*, "to hammer"

10. brothel
    (a) from Old English *brucan*, "to use"
    (b) from "*brotherly* (love)"
    (c) from Old English *breothan*, "to go to ruin"

---

Correct answers: 1 (a), 2 (b), 3 (a), 4 (a), 5 (b), 6 (c), 7 (a), 8 (c), 9 (b), 10 (c)

Your score: _____
(10–9 correct: superb; 8–6 correct: good; 5–4 correct: fair)

# Questions, Questions
### by Gershon K. Gershon

The English word *quaint* (from Old French *cointe*, "clever") has or at one time had which of the following meanings?

1. agreeable, amiable, affable
2. elegant, neat, trim, spruce
3. pleasingly odd or unusual
4. clever, cunning
5. gracious, gentle
6. pretty, handsome
7. attractive because of an old-fashioned daintiness
8. proper
9. prudent
10. discreet
11. knowing, wise
12. happy

The answer is: all the meanings. (The primary meanings today are 3 and 7.)

---

What do these words have in common?

1. V-bomb
2. brownout
3. doodle bug
4. Seabees
5. globaloney
6. island-hopping
7. de-Nazification
8. pedal pusher
9. DDT
10. jet plane
11. sky train
12. newsmap

191

13. pesticide      16. streptomycin

14. buzz-bomb      17. displaced person

15. flying jeep      18. bobby soxer

The answer is: They are among the many terms that were coined or came into usage while Franklin D. Roosevelt was President (1933–45).

*Mr. Gershon is a much-published historian and wordsmith living in New York City.*

# Chapter XIII

## Vocabulary Test No. 37

Which word or phrase is nearest in meaning to each of the following headwords?

1. allegory   (al'əgōr'ē)
   - (a) result
   - (b) figurative treatment of one subject under the guise of another
   - (c) treaty
   - (d) alliteration in a foreign language

2. rodomontade   (rod'əmontād')
   - (a) vainglorious boasting or bragging
   - (b) public exhibition of cowboy skills
   - (c) ornate or florid message
   - (d) signal received and understood

3. flummery   (flum'ərē)
   - (a) vacuity
   - (b) high wind
   - (c) suitable praise
   - (d) foolish humbug

4. to enucleate   (inōō'klē·āt')
   - (a) to remove (something) from an enveloping cover
   - (b) to read from the pulpit in a Protestant church
   - (c) to make inflammatory comments
   - (d) to prohibit by injunction

5. quixotic   (kwiksot'ik)
   (a) traveling at the fastest possible speed
   (b) abandoning an effort
   (c) extravagantly chivalrous and idealistic
   (d) of doubtful honesty

6. empathy   (em'pəthē)
   (a) familiar route
   (b) identification with feelings or thoughts of another person
   (c) magic spell
   (d) history of a dynasty

7. palaver   (pəlav'ər)
   (a) profuse and idle talk
   (b) the "talk" of ducks
   (c) one's best friend
   (d) expert in everyday matters

8. perspicuous   (pərspik'yōō·əs)
   (a) clear in expression or statement
   (b) excreting much body vapor during interrogation
   (c) appealing to reason or understanding
   (d) justifying through religious belief

9. latent   (lāt'ʾnt)
   (a) early in pregnancy
   (b) recently
   (c) potential but not visible
   (d) on the verge of announcement

10. polyglot   (pol'ēglot')
    (a) voracious individual
    (b) many-sided geometrical figure
    (c) paralyzed veteran
    (d) person who speaks several languages

---

Correct answers: 1 (b), 2 (a), 3 (d), 4 (a), 5 (c), 6 (b), 7 (a), 8 (a), 9 (c), 10 (d)

Your score:_____
(10–8 correct: superb; 7–5 correct: good; 4–3 correct: fair)

# Over There

See how well you know your British English.

| BRITISH ENGLISH | AMERICAN ENGLISH |
|---|---|
| 1. bobby | _____ |
| 2. ack-ack | _____ |
| 3. yeoman | _____ |
| 4. zebra cross-ing | _____ |
| 5. tiffin | _____ |
| 6. toffee | _____ |
| 7. constable | _____ |
| 8. minster | _____ |
| 9. tea | _____ |
| 10. petrol | _____ |
| 11. gazette | _____ |
| 12. sweep | _____ |
| 13. preparatory school | _____ |
| 14. darned! | _____ |
| 15. accumulator | _____ |
| 16. whilst | _____ |
| 17. back bench | _____ |
| 18. almoner | _____ |

19. lorry           _____

20. ladder (speak-     _____
      ing of fabric)

---

Correct answers: 1. policeman; 2. British radio code for A.A., that is, antiaircraft; 3. formerly freeholder ranking below the gentry; 4. safety crossing on a street, marked with painted white stripes; 5. lunch; 6. taffy; 7. policeman; 8. monastery church; 9. late-afternoon meal; 10. gasoline; 11. official government publication; 12. chimney sweeper; 13. private elementary school; 14. damned!; 15. storage battery or cell; 16. while; 17. in the House of Commons, row of seats that may be occupied by any member; 18. social worker in a hospital; 19. truck; 20. run (as in a stocking)

Your score:_____
(20–18 correct: superb; 17–14 correct: good; 13–11 correct: fair)

# Vocabulary Test No. 38

Which word or phrase is nearest in meaning to each of the following headwords?

1. fauna (fô'nə)
   (a) debris found in streams and brooks
   (b) animals of a given region or period
   (c) half-human deity with the hind legs of a goat
   (d) young leaves on a fern

2. hirsute (hûr'soot)
   (a) fortuitous
   (b) suitable for a single purpose
   (c) unusually hairy
   (d) threatening

3. incarnate (inkär'nit)
   (a) having a bodily, esp. a human, form
   (b) flesh-eating
   (c) keel-like
   (d) having fragrant flowers of various colors

4. swain (swān)
   (a) cygnet
   (b) lover or gallant
   (c) small bird having long wings and a forked tail, noted for its swift, graceful flight
   (d) large mop for cleaning decks

5. sonorous (sənôr'əs)
   (a) giving a deep, full sound
   (b) calming or mitigating
   (c) extremely drowsy
   (d) capable of being dissolved

197

6. **fulsome**  (foŏl′səm)
   - (a) feeling "stuffed," as after a rich meal
   - (b) wholesome
   - (c) frivolous
   - (d) offensive to good taste, esp. as being excessive

7. **redolent**  (red′°lənt)
   - (a) mournfully sad
   - (b) having a pleasant odor
   - (c) full of or causing pain or sorrow
   - (d) inactive or stagnating, as business or the arts

8. **hedonism**  (hēd′°niz′əm)
   - (a) hatred of everything
   - (b) devotion to pleasure as a way of life
   - (c) careful attention
   - (d) flight pattern at a very low altitude

9. **acrid**  (ak′rid)
   - (a) slightly sour
   - (b) friendless
   - (c) sharp or biting to the taste or smell
   - (d) bloody

10. **servile**  (sûr′vil)
    - (a) in the morning
    - (b) tabled
    - (c) vituperative
    - (d) slavishly obedient

---

Correct answers: 1 (b), 2 (c), 3 (a), 4 (b), 5 (a), 6 (d), 7 (b), 8 (b), 9 (c), 10 (d)

Your score: _____
(10–8 correct: superb; 7–5 correct: good; 4–3 correct: fair)

198

# Fill In the Blanks

Example:
a person who affects to possess great wisdom:
w __ __e a c __e

The answer is "wiseacre."

1. to behave snobbishly toward (someone):
   __p s t __ __ __

2. the track or trail of a wild animal: __ __o o __

3. the philosophical doctrine that no knowledge is trustworthy: __ __ __p t i __ __ __ __

4. an act of anointing, esp. as a medical treatment or religious rite; hypocritical or affected earnestness, esp. in language: u __ __ __ __ __ __n

5. indeed (archaic): __o __s __ __t h

6. very loud: f o r __i __ __ __ __ __

7. unduly distended or swollen; inflated or overblown, as writing: __ __ __g __d

8. a disease of rabbits, etc., transmitted to human beings by insects: __u l a r e m __ __

9. a container for carrying the Eucharist to the sick: __y __

10. to pillage (a place) after capture: __ __c __

---

Correct answers: 1. upstage 2. spoor 3. skepticism 4. unction 5. forsooth 6. fortissimo 7. turgid 8. tularemia 9. pyx 10. sack

Your score: _____
(10–9 correct: superb; 8–6 correct: good; 5–4 correct: fair)

# Vocabulary Test No. 39

Which word or phrase is nearest in meaning to each of the following headwords?

1. **to adumbrate** (adum′brāt)
   (a) to be obstinate
   (b) to blossom
   (c) to adore
   (d) to foreshadow

2. **cusp** (kusp)
   (a) lip
   (b) edge
   (c) pointed end (as on the crown of a tooth)
   (d) curse word

3. **tendril** (ten′dril)
   (a) rock music
   (b) coil-like part of a climbing plant that winds around its supports
   (c) person who abstains totally from alcoholic drinks
   (d) cord of dense, tough tissue connecting a muscle with a bone

4. **flange** (flanj)
   (a) projecting rim on a pipe
   (b) side of an animal or a human between the ribs and hip
   (c) long, lashlike appendage serving as an organ of locomotion in certain reproductive bodies, bacteria, protozoa, etc.
   (d) whip or scourge

5. **protuberance** (prōtoo′bərəns)
   (a) pocket on the abdomen of certain animals, as kangaroos, in which the young are carried

    (b) discontinued session (of the British Parliament)
    (c) thing or part that thrusts out
    (d) the study of noses, human and animal

6. **wizened** (wiz′ənd)
    (a) magical
    (b) shriveled and dried up, as from age
    (c) in intense grievous distress
    (d) swollen (as from a growth in the stomach)

7. **unctuous** (ungk′chōō·əs)
    (a) indisputably good
    (b) hypocritically smooth or suave
    (c) not subject to conditions
    (d) greasy

8. **dormer** (dôr′mər)
    (a) sleeping mouse
    (b) snout on a polar bear
    (c) vertical window in a projection built out from a sloping roof
    (d) wedding night (slang)

9. **chaplet** (chap′lit)
    (a) knitted legging worn on each calf by a cowboy
    (b) cross that towers over a chapel
    (c) small condominium
    (d) wreath or garland for the head

10. **crenel** (kren′′l)
    (a) hooped underskirt
    (b) gong
    (c) mouth of a cannon
    (d) open space between the merlons of a battlement

---

Correct answers: 1 (d), 2 (c), 3 (b), 4 (a), 5 (c), 6 (b), 7 (b), 8 (c), 9 (d), 10 (d)

Your score: _____
(10–8 correct: superb; 7–5 correct: good; 4–3 correct: fair)

# Word Roots, Test M

Each of the following ten words stems from one of the three sources shown. Mark the correct answer.

1. coda
   (a) from Latin *codex*, "wooden writing tablet"
   (b) from Spanish *caudillo*, "head (of the state)"
   (c) from Latin *cauda*, "tail"

2. ocarina
   (a) from Italian *oca*, "goose"
   (b) from Latin *occludere*, "to shut up"
   (c) from Latin *occidentalis*, "western"

3. baritone
   (a) from Latin *barca*, "boat"
   (b) from Greek *barytonos*, "deep-sounding"
   (c) from Late Latin *barcaniare*, "to haggle"

4. praise
   (a) from Old French *preisier*, "to prize"
   (b) from Latin *praesto*, "at hand"
   (c) from Latin *prehendere*, "to seize"

5. to span
   (a) from Latin *expendere*, "to pay out"
   (b) from Dutch *spannen*, "to unite"
   (c) from Dutch *spatten*, "to burst, to spout"

6. torpedo
   (a) Latin *torpedin*, for "numbness, listlessness"
   (b) from Spanish *toreador*, "bullfighter"
   (c) from French *touché*, "touched"

7. **orbit**
   (a) from Sir William N. M. *Orpen* (1878–1931)
   (b) from Greek *orchis*, "testicle"
   (c) from Latin *orbita*, "wheel track"

8. **orang-utan**
   (a) Malay for "man of the forest"
   (b) from Latin *oris*, "mouth"
   (c) from Latin *orans*, "praying," plus *uterus*, "womb"

9. **dolomite**
   (a) from Old English *dal*, "portion"
   (b) from the French geologist *Dolomieu* (1750–1801)
   (c) from Latin *dolor*, "sorrow"

10. **plume**
   (a) from Middle English *plompe*, "dull"
   (b) from *plunder*
   (c) from Latin *pluma*, "down"

---

Correct answers: 1 (c), 2 (a), 3 (b), 4 (a), 5 (b), 6 (a), 7 (c), 8 (a), 9 (b), 10 (c)

Your score: _____
(10–9 correct: superb; 8–6 correct: good; 5–4 correct: fair)

# Lassoing a Tough Critter

### by J. L. Dillard

Like most interesting etymologies, that of *larrupin'* is more than a little questionable. The traditional dictionaries, culminating more or less in *Webster's Third*, label it "perh[aps] imit[ative]," a derivation to which anyone who can imagine a whip flashing through the air with the sound "larrup" is welcome. The *Oxford English Dictionary* quotes an 1825 guess deriving the verbal base from *lee-rope*.

In the meaning "whip," the word invaded the Eastern seaboard and produced the nickname of "Larrupin' Lou" Gehrig, the slugging New York Yankee first baseman whose drives were whiplike. In the South and West, the dominant sense is now "excellent" or even "tasty." Ramon Adams's *Western Words* records both "*larrup*. A cowboy name for molasses. To strike, to thrash" and "*larrupin' truck*. A cowboy's name for anything he considers great stuff." A late informant stressed how, in syrup-making in East Texas, the "whiplike" strands of syrup that spilled over from the superior top layer of the ribbon cane syrup were unusually tasty.

It appears plausible that the maritime word established itself on the Eastern seaboard without any association with sugar cane, molasses, or syrup, that it acquired that relationship when imported, along with sugar cane, to the Gulf states, and that it then spread across the Louisiana border to Texas and west with the cattle trade. It has been called "of Southern origin, widely current in California" and treated as characteristic of Snake County, Missouri. Informal and homey associations seem to prevent anyone's suspecting the very widespread and perhaps originally nautical distribution of the word.

*Dr. Dillard is Professor of English at Northwestern State University of Louisiana.*

# Chapter XIV

## Vocabulary Test No. 40

Which word or phrase is nearest in meaning to each of the following headwords?

1. **gargantuan** (gärgan′ch͞oo·ən)
   - (a) of enormous size or capacity
   - (b) apelike
   - (c) stiff-necked
   - (d) spiritless

2. **atom** (at′əm)
   - (a) largest unit in nature
   - (b) anything extremely small
   - (c) huge explosion
   - (d) a wasting away

3. **tumescent** (t͞oomes′ənt)
   - (a) swelling
   - (b) bombastic
   - (c) greatly agitated
   - (d) giving off great odor

4. **defalcation** (dē′falkā′shən)
   - (a) congenital lying
   - (b) dissemination of a deceptive or misleading idea
   - (c) lack of conformity to truth or fact
   - (d) misappropriation of money held by an official

5. corpulence   (kôr′pyələns)
   (a) fleshy fatness
   (b) hock of ham
   (c) the body politic
   (d) quarrel or fight

6. lacuna   (ləkyōō′nə)
   (a) empty or missing part, esp. in an ancient manuscript
   (b) deafness
   (c) lack of spirit or interest
   (d) sweetness

7. to dilate   (dīlāt′)
   (a) to tolerate tardiness
   (b) to make thinner or weaker by the addition of water
   (c) to make wider or larger
   (d) to expel two similar complements of chromosomes

8. apogee   (ap′əjē)
   (a) nervous breakdown
   (b) highest point or part
   (c) person who makes a defense
   (d) departure from one's religion or cause

9. behemoth   (bihē′məth)
   (a) largest known bat
   (b) huge animal
   (c) winner of a wrestling championship
   (d) obligation

10. to incrassate   (inkras′āt)
   (a) to cover with a crust or hard coating
   (b) to oppress (women)
   (c) to be willing to believe or trust
   (d) to thicken

---

Correct answers: 1 (a), 2 (b), 3 (a), 4 (d), 5 (a), 6 (a), 7 (c),
8 (b), 9 (b), 10 (d)

Your score: _____
(10–8 correct: superb; 7–5 correct: good; 4–3 correct: fair)

# Eponyms

The items at the left refer to proper names; the items at the right define words or phrases that are derived from these proper names. Match them.

Example:

a town in Belgium _____    a large, cylindrical canvas bag for carrying personal effects

The answer is "duffel bag" (Duffel).

1. a hill in ancient Rome _____

2. a former capital of China _____

3. a village in West Germany _____

4. a fictional lover _____

5. a boy's given name _____

6. a county in England _____

7. a city in Scotland _____

8. a U.S. baby doctor _____

9. an eighteenth-century judge _____

10. a city in West Germany _____

(a) to hang or otherwise kill (a person) by mob action and without legal authority

(b) the official residence of a sovereign or bishop; any large and stately building

(c) a farm or work horse

(d) a man's felt hat with a soft crown dented lengthwise and a slightly rolled brim

(e) a firm, durable, yellow or buff fabric

(f) a natural effervescent mineral water containing common salt

(g) a light, four-wheeled, two-seated carriage

(h) to make love without serious intentions (said of a man)

(i) a skin test to determine immunity to diphtheria

(j) having a pattern of colorful and minutely detailed figures

---

Correct answers: 1 (b) palace (the hill Palatium), 2 (e) nankeen (Nanking), 3 (f) Seltzer (Nieder-Selters), 4 (h) to philander (Philandros), 5 (c) dobbin (diminutive of Robert), 6 (g) surrey (Surrey), 7 (j) paisley (Paisley), 8 (i) Schick test (Bela Schick, 1877–1967), 9 (a) to lynch (Charles Lynch, 1736–96), 10 (d) homburg (Bad Homburg)

Your score: _____
(10–9 correct: superb; 8–6 correct: good; 5–4 correct: fair)

# Vocabulary Test No. 41

Which word or phrase is nearest in meaning to each of the following headwords?

1. **animadversion** (an'əmadvûr'zhən)
   (a) criticism
   (b) cloth or paper headrest protecting chairs from oily hair
   (c) Gandhi's attitude toward nubile, teenage secretaries
   (d) the other team in a contest

2. **anhedonia** (an'hēdō'nē-ə)
   (a) trumpet blast that crumbles walls
   (b) original term for flea-flicker play in professional football
   (c) elation over unique sports play
   (d) absence of the capacity to experience pleasure

3. **uxorious** (uksōr'ē-əs)
   (a) excessive
   (b) foolishly fond of or submissive toward one's wife
   (c) three-masted
   (d) T-shaped, as the yoke of oxen

4. **fatuous** (fach'ōō·əs)
   (a) overweight
   (b) complacently foolish or silly
   (c) nautical
   (d) pertaining to hydrocarbons

5. **fecund** (fē'kund)
   (a) favored
   (b) pertaining to the body's eliminations
   (c) prolific or fruitful
   (d) seeded

6. pejorative   (pijôr′ətiv)
   (a) circling the Earth
   (b) minority-controlled
   (c) disparaging
   (d) crushing, as an argument

7. myriad   (mir′ē·əd)
   (a) isotope of hydrogen having an atomic weight of 3
   (b) an indefinitely great number
   (c) three slaves to an oar in a triptych
   (d) plural possessive when a one-syllable word ends in "s"

8. symbiosis   (sim′bī·ō′sis)
   (a) cancer of the liver
   (b) battle formation established by the queen ant
   (c) the living together of two dissimilar organisms, esp. when mutually beneficial
   (d) plausibility

9. to lallygag   (lol′ēgag′)
   (a) to have candy caught in the throat (Yiddish)
   (b) to idle or loaf
   (c) to zigzag
   (d) to hum

10. endemic   (endem′ik)
   (a) peculiar to a particular people or locality, as a disease
   (b) courageous and resolute
   (c) pertaining to or marked by fever of more than 103°F
   (d) injected into the rectum

---

Correct answers: 1 (a), 2 (d), 3 (b), 4 (b), 5 (c), 6 (c), 7 (b), 8 (c), 9 (b), 10 (a)

Your score:_____
(10–8 correct: superb; 7–5 correct: good; 4–3 correct: fair)

# There *Is* a Word for It

Example:
a clever but specious argument: s_____

The answer is "sophism."

1. Protestant denomination founded in England in the seventeenth century, opposed to oath-taking and war:
   S_____ o_____
   F_____

2. a mimeographed periodical distributed by science-fiction or comic-strip devotees: f_____

3. a door consisting of two units horizontally divided so that they can be opened separately:
   D_____ d_____

4. a long strip of cloth wound round the lower leg:
   p_____

5. sentimental in an objectionably excessive way:
   m_____

6. the branch of mechanics that deals with pure motion, without reference to the masses or forces involved in it:
   k_____

7. of or describing witty, amusing rogues or their adventures: p_____

8. a box or trough from which horses or cattle eat:
   m_____

9. temperamentally not speaking much:
   t_____

10. the science dealing with the effects of space travel upon life: b _____

_____

Correct answers: 1. Society of Friends 2. fanzine 3. Dutch door 4. puttee 5. mawkish 6. kinematics 7. picaresque 8. manger 9. taciturn 10. bioastronautics

Your score:_____
(10–9 correct: superb; 8–6 correct: good; 5–4 correct: fair)

# Vocabulary Test No. 42

Which word or phrase is nearest in meaning to each of the following headwords from the diaries of Igor Stravinsky's Boswell, Robert Craft?

1. **detritus**  (ditrī′təs)
   - (a) burned-out forest
   - (b) material broken away from a mass
   - (c) nymph of the woods
   - (d) dessert prepared with hot or savory seasoning

2. **anchorite**  (an̂g′kərīt′)
   - (a) place for anchoring a vessel
   - (b) hermit, esp. of the early Christian church
   - (c) automaton in the form of a human being
   - (d) very low degree of reverberation

3. **dhoti**  (dō′tē)
   - (a) Arabian one-sail ship
   - (b) loincloth worn by Hindu men in India
   - (c) mixture of tallow and oil used in dressing leather
   - (d) territory ruled over by a duchess

4. **pubescent**  (pyo͞obes′ənt)
   - (a) off bounds to minors
   - (b) periodical or regular
   - (c) expired, as a copyright
   - (d) arriving or arrived at the age when one is capable of sexual reproduction

5. **scatology**  (skətol′əjē)
   - (a) preoccupation with excrement or obscenity
   - (b) random distribution
   - (c) mental state of a person incapable of serious, connected thought
   - (d) the study of bebop

213

6. **analogue**   (an′ᵊlôg′)
   (a) that which has resemblance to something else
   (b) rectal surgery
   (c) the separating of any entity into its constituent elements
   (d) the methods of anarchists

7. **anachronism**   (ənak′rəniz′əm)
   (a) South African boat, usually of more than thirty feet
   (b) condition of a person undergoing psychoanalysis
   (c) person or thing that is chronologically out of place
   (d) dysfunction of time

8. **apparition**   (ap′ərish′ən)
   (a) segregation of blacks in South Africa
   (b) land or revenue granted to a member of a royal family
   (c) reform movement
   (d) ghostly appearance

9. **fasces**   (fas′ēz)
   (a) bundle of rods containing an ax, borne before Roman magistrates as an emblem of authority
   (b) fetid situation
   (c) the quality of being excessively critical or demanding
   (d) interest or curiosity

10. **knobkerrie**   (nob′ker′ē)
   (a) short, heavy stick used by southern African peoples for striking and throwing
   (b) knocker on the front door of colonial mansions in New England
   (c) wild fruit found principally along the Gulf of Mexico
   (d) one word for "burning your bridges behind you"

---

Correct answers: 1 (b), 2 (b), 3 (b), 4 (d), 5 (a), 6 (a), 7 (c), 8 (d), 9 (a), 10 (a)

Your score: _____
(10–8 correct: superb; 7–5 correct: good; 4–3 correct: fair)

# Word Roots, Test N

Each of the following ten words stems from one of the three sources shown. Mark the correct answer.

1. discreet
   (a) from Medieval Latin *discretus*, "separate"
   (b) from Latin *discrepans*, "out of tune"
   (c) from Latin *discrimen*, "distinction"

2. jovial
   (a) from Latin *jubilum*, "shout"
   (b) from Latin *jovialis*, "of the planet Jupiter" (supposed to have a benign influence on humans)
   (c) from Old French *juster*, "to joust"

3. mature
   (a) from the Hollywood star Victor *Mature*
   (b) from Latin *matrix*, "womb"
   (c) from Latin *maturus*, "ripe"

4. funicular—worked by a rope, as a railway
   (a) from Latin *infundibulum*, "funnel"
   (b) from Latin *fundamentum*, "foundation"
   (c) from Latin *funis*, "cord"

5. helm
   (a) from Old English *helma*, "rudder"
   (b) from Old English *helpan*, "help"
   (c) from German *Helm*, "head cover"

6. to peel
   (a) from Latin *pilare*, "to remove hair from"
   (b) from Middle English *pepe*, "peep"
   (c) from Latin *pejorare*, "to make worse"

7. **dismal**
   (a) from Latin *dies mali*, "unlucky days"
   (b) from the *Dismal* Swamp in Virginia and North Carolina
   (c) from Latin *decima*, "tenth"

8. **gambol**
   (a) from Greek *gametes*, "husband"
   (b) from Middle French *gambade*, "leap"
   (c) from Italian *gambetto*, "act of tripping"

9. **geezer**
   (a) from Latin *genus*, "kind"
   (b) from Middle English *gasen*, "to gaze, to stare"
   (c) probably from Scottish *guiser*, "person in disguise"

10. **logistics**
   (a) from the Scandinavian mythological *Logi*, who defeated Loki in an eating contest
   (b) from French *loger*, "to lodge"
   (c) from *logging*

---

Correct answers: 1 (a), 2 (b), 3 (c), 4 (c), 5 (a), 6 (a), 7 (a), 8 (b), 9 (c), 10 (b)

Your score: _____
(10–9 correct: superb; 8–6 correct: good; 5–4 correct: fair)

# Mafia—Perhaps
## by Robert J. Di Pietro

In the interest of historical accuracy, it must be said that no one is certain how the term *Mafia* arose. One of the popular etymologies is tracing it as an acronym from the phrase "*M*orte *a*lla *F*rancia *I*talia *A*nela"—"Italy longs for (or strives for) death to France." However, no one can be certain that the word did not already exist in Sicilian dialect before it became a slogan for Italian unity. The Risorgimento was a time for Italians to develop patriotic slogans with partly veiled meanings. The name of the composer Guiseppe Verdi, for example, came to stand for "*V*ittorio *E*mmanuele, *Re d'I*talia"—"Victor Emmanuel, king of Italy." Any Italian firebrand caught writing "VERDI" on a wall in Austrian-occupied Italy could always claim that he was only showing his admiration for the great composer. The word *Mafia* could have been put to a similar use.

One suggestion is that *Mafia* came from an Arabic word, *maehfil*, meaning originally "secret meeting place." This etymology is supported by the known presence of Arabs in Sicily during the period just before the Normans arrived. The original meaning of the adjective derived from *Mafia*, *mafioso*, could then be placed in the context of one who is haughty and secretive at the same time. Remember that the original members of the *Mafia* were noblemen. The feminine form of the adjective, by the way, also exists in Sicilian, *mafiosa*, and is a compliment to a young lady. Basically, it means a woman or girl who is "spunky" and not afraid to assert herself. The idiom *far la mafia* is found in standard Italian as well and means to be ostentatious and disdainful.

It is not easy to lift the shroud of mystery that surrounds the origins of the *Mafia* and the etymology of the term. The many attempts made to explain its meaning would best be characterized in Italian as *forse veri, ma ad ogni modo, ben trovati!*—"true, perhaps, but, in any event, well-found (or well-invented)."

*Dr. Di Pietro is Chairman of the Department of Languages and Literatures at the University of Delaware.*

# Chapter XV

## Vocabulary Test No. 43

Which word or phrase is nearest in meaning to each of the following headwords?

1. **shibboleth** (s̲h̲ib′əlit̲h̲)
   - (a) foaming of the mouth, esp. among seekers of political power
   - (b) peculiarity of speech that distinguishes a particular set of persons
   - (c) chief law-enforcement officer in northern African countries
   - (d) wise saying that, because it is indeed true, becomes a cliché

2. **cynic** (sin′ik)
   - (a) center of attention
   - (b) resident of an island country in the Mediterranean
   - (c) person who believes that only selfishness motivates human actions
   - (d) owner of a brothel in Turkey

3. **quintessence** (kwintes′əns)
   - (a) combination of five ingredients that makes the perfect aphrodisiac
   - (b) official management of a sovereign's living quarters
   - (c) the most perfect embodiment of something
   - (d) popular word to describe the five roads that led into Keifeng, once China's capital

4. **ambrosia** (ambrō'zhə)
   - (a) combination or mixture
   - (b) love potion
   - (c) food and drink of the gods
   - (d) uncertainty or fluctuation caused by inability to make a choice

5. **portmanteau** (pōrtman'tō)
   - (a) leather trunk that opens into two halves
   - (b) second half of a double streetcar
   - (c) overseer on a wharf, usually in Southeast Asia
   - (d) priceless champagne from grapes grown in southeast France

6. **stentorian** (stentōr'ē·ən)
   - (a) of the Roman Senate
   - (b) charming but evil
   - (c) extended
   - (d) very loud or strong in sound

7. **dirge** (dûrj)
   - (a) baleful influence
   - (b) song in commemoration of the dead
   - (c) predetermined course of events
   - (d) uninhibited passion

8. **tandem** (tan'dəm)
   - (a) skinning (an animal) alive
   - (b) devoted to luxury and pleasure
   - (c) afraid of one's own shadow
   - (d) one following the other

9. **gauche** (gōsh)
   - (a) courting the votes of Mexican immigrants
   - (b) lacking social grace or tact
   - (c) pertaining to the hammer used by the Speaker to call the House of Representatives to order
   - (d) amazed by a sudden revelation

10. **umbrage** (um'brij)
    (a) shelter from the media, preferably a hideaway
    (b) resentful displeasure or personal offense
    (c) shady side of politics
    (d) money passed under the table in a scene recorded
        secretly on videotape

---

Correct answers: 1 (b), 2 (c), 3 (c), 4 (c), 5 (a), 6 (d), 7 (b),
8 (d), 9 (b), 10 (b)

Your score: _____
(10–8 correct: superb; 7–5 correct: good; 4–3 correct: fair)

# In Words

These ten "in-" words came in in one of the time slots at the right.

1. "incontrovertible" was coined _____
   - (a) between 1850 and 1900.
   - (b) between 1901 and 1950.
   - (c) between 1600 and 1700.

2. "industrialism" was coined _____
   - (a) in 1911.
   - (b) in 1823.
   - (c) in 1930.

3. "infinitesimal" was coined _____
   - (a) between 1900 and 1950.
   - (b) between 1650 and 1750.
   - (c) between 1750 and 1850.

4. "insecurity" was coined _____
   - (a) between 1900 and 1950.
   - (b) between 1800 and 1900.
   - (c) between 1600 and 1700.

5. "insulin" was coined _____
   - (a) in 1921.
   - (b) in 1886.
   - (c) in 1948.

6. "intellectualism" was coined _____
   - (a) in 1803.
   - (b) in 1903.
   - (c) in 1703.

7. "intensify" was coined _____
   - (a) between 1850 and 1950.
   - (b) between 1750 and 1849.
   - (c) between 1650 and 1749.

8. "intensity" was coined _____
   (a) between 1750 and 1850.
   (b) between 1900 and 1950.
   (c) between 1600 and 1700.

9. "international" was coined _____
   (a) in 1880.
   (b) in 1902.
   (c) in 1780.

10. "invertebrate" was coined _____
    (a) in 1705.
    (b) in 1805.
    (c) in 1905.

---

Correct answers:

1(c) By the English physician and writer Sir Thomas Browne (1605–82).

2(b) By the comte de Saint-Simon (1760–1825)—*industrialisme*.

3(b) By the German philosopher and mathematician G. W. von Leibniz (1646–1716), from Latin *infinitus*, "boundless."

4(c) By Sir Thomas Browne—see 1(c).

5(a) By Sir E. A. W. Sharpey (1850–1935).

6(a) By the German philosopher F. W. J. von Schelling (1775–1854), from Latin *intellectualis*, "relating to understanding"—*Intellektualismus*.

7(b) By the English poet and philosopher S. T. Coleridge (1772–1834).

8(c) By the English physicist Robert Boyle (1627–91).

9(c) By the English reformer and philosopher Jeremy Bentham (1748–1832).

10(b) By the French naturalist G. L. C. F. D. Cuvier (1769–1832)—*invertébré*.

Your score: _____

(10–8 correct: superb; 7–5 correct: good; 4–3 correct: fair)

# Vocabulary Test No. 44

Which word or phrase is nearest in meaning to each of the following headwords?

1. **anagram** (an'əgram')
   (a) word formed by transposing the letters of another word
   (b) word formed by smoke signals
   (c) strongest vitamin that can safely be given a toddler
   (d) word opposite in meaning to another

2. **synapse** (sin'aps)
   (a) semen ejaculated during sleep
   (b) saliva mixed with mucus
   (c) area between two nerve cells where impulses are transmitted
   (d) assembly of church officials or delegates

3. **syllogism** (sil'əjiz'əm)
   (a) pointless political position
   (b) deductive argument in which a conclusion is supported by two premises
   (c) outline or other brief statement, esp. of a course of study
   (d) sublime scientific argument

4. **heuristic** (hyŏŏris'tik)
   (a) long-bearded
   (b) encouraging the student to discover for himself or herself
   (c) pertaining to the point at which two computer bytes come together
   (d) different in kind

5. **inductive** (induk′tiv)
   (a) enlisted in U.S. armed service
   (b) seductive
   (c) supplied through a pipe line
   (d) pertaining to roundabout logical reasoning

6. **empiricism** (empir′isiz′əm)
   (a) far-ranging political power
   (b) royal arrogance
   (c) doctrine that all knowledge is derived from sense experience
   (d) acquisition of overseas colonies

7. **mnemonic** (nēmon′ik)
   (a) forming a new word from the initial letters of an organization
   (b) intended to aid the memory
   (c) manic depressive
   (d) living "in the tent of wickedness"

8. **parsimony** (pär′səmō′nē)
   (a) extreme or excessive frugality
   (b) estate inherited from one's father or ancestors
   (c) jargon
   (d) garden herb with aromatic leaves; used to garnish food

9. **perception** (pərsep′shən)
   (a) example of excellence
   (b) mental recognition
   (c) upside-down vision
   (d) extinction or oblivion

10. **hypothesis** (hīpoth′isis)
    (a) two-foot-long needle used to drug thick-skinned mammals of Africa and India before transporting them to safe preserves
    (b) exaggerated position in a college senior's term paper, to insure a passing grade
    (c) testable assumption
    (d) result of having too much sugar in the blood

**Correct answers:** 1 (a), 2 (c), 3 (b), 4 (b), 5 (d), 6 (c), 7 (b), 8 (a), 9 (b), 10 (c)

**Your score:** _____
(10–8 correct: superb; 7–5 correct: good; 4–3 correct: fair)

# What Our Presidents Didn't Know

Which President—while he was in office—did not know this expression because it was coined or came into usage during the *next* administration? (See the example on page 42.)

1. bread (money): _____
2. southpaw: _____
3. Kodak: _____
4. book matches: _____
5. junk mail: _____
6. head shrinker: _____
7. Eskimo pie: _____
8. Penicillin: _____
9. pantyhose: _____
10. dynamite: _____

---

Correct answers: 1. Herbert Hoover, 1929–33; 2. Chester A. Arthur, 1881–85; 3. Chester A. Arthur, 1881–85; 4. Grover Cleveland, 1885–89; 5. Harry S Truman, 1945–53; 6. Harry S Truman, 1945–53; 7. Woodrow Wilson, 1913–21; 8. Warren Harding, 1921–23; 9. Dwight Eisenhower, 1953–61; 10. James Buchanan, 1857–61

Your score:_____
(10–8 correct: superb; 7–4 correct: good; 3–2 correct: fair)

# Vocabulary Test No. 45

Which word or phrase is nearest in meaning to each of the following headwords?

1. **audacious** (ôdā′shəs)
   - (a) inspiring awe and reverence
   - (b) extremely daring, or insolent
   - (c) factually accurate or reliable
   - (d) severely stern or strict, as in manner

2. **redoubtable** (ridou′təbəl)
   - (a) to be feared
   - (b) said in protest, objection, or disapproval
   - (c) made more tense
   - (d) mild, compassionate, or forgiving

3. **sanguine** (saṅg′gwin)
   - (a) cheerful and hopeful
   - (b) like or befitting a saint
   - (c) fearful or nervous
   - (d) capable of being held, maintained, or defended

4. **roseate** (rō′zē·it)
   - (a) gullible
   - (b) dissipated, lecherous
   - (c) optimistic or promising
   - (d) shaped roughly

5. **to affiance** (əfī′əns)
   - (a) to treasure
   - (b) to oppose
   - (c) to make rich
   - (d) to betroth

228

6. ogre   (ō'gər)
   (a) dull mind
   (b) monstrously cruel person
   (c) appropriate time
   (d) glance

7. poltroon   (poltrōōn')
   (a) cuspidor
   (b) wretched coward
   (c) dark-colored North Atlantic food fish of the cod family
   (d) high or chief priest

8. to envisage   (enviz'ij)
   (a) to imagine and visualize
   (b) to become distended with blood
   (c) to face down
   (d) to deprive of strength or vigor

9. intrepid   (intrep'id)
   (a) undergoing a long journey
   (b) having the quality of travesty
   (c) flexing a muscle
   (d) absolutely fearless or dauntless

10. obdurate   (ob'dōōrit)
   (a) resulting from public censure
   (b) halting
   (c) stubborn, unyielding
   (d) blotted out

_____

Correct answers: 1 (b), 2 (a), 3 (a), 4 (c), 5 (d), 6 (b), 7 (b), 8 (a), 9 (d), 10 (c)

Your score: _____
(10–8 correct: superb; 7–5 correct: good; 4–3 correct: fair)

# Word Roots, Test O

Each of the following ten words stems from one of the three sources shown. Mark the correct answer.

1. **vendetta**
   - (a) from Latin *Venereus*, "venereal"
   - (b) from Latin *venia*, "pardon"
   - (c) from Latin *vindicta*, "vengeance"

2. **viscera**
   - (a) from Latin *viscus*, "organ"
   - (b) from Latin *visum*, "appearance"
   - (c) from Old High German *wisunt*, "bison"

3. **obstetrics**
   - (a) from Latin *obstetrix*, "midwife"
   - (b) from Latin *obstrepere*, "to make a noise"
   - (c) from Latin *obstinare*, "to persist in"

4. **invoice**
   - (a) from Middle French *envois*, "messages"
   - (b) from "to *invoke*"
   - (c) from Latin *investire*, "to clothe in"

5. **to deplore**
   - (a) from "to *deploy*"
   - (b) from Latin *deplorare*, "to wail"
   - (c) from Latin *deplere*, "to empty"

6. **mosaic**
   - (a) from the Hebrew patriarch *Moses*
   - (b) from Old English *mos*, "moss"
   - (c) from Greek *mouseios*, "of the Muses"

7. **to ostracize**
   - (a) from Greek *osmos*, "push"

230

(b) from Greek *ostrakon*, "tile used in voting"
(c) from Latin *ostendere*, "to expose"

8. rosary
   (a) from Latin *rosarium*, "rose garden"
   (b) from Latin *ros marinus*, "marine dew"
   (c) from *rousing*

9. lanyard
   (a) from Old French *lasniere*, "thong"
   (b) from Walter Savage *Landor* (1775–1864)
   (c) from *longwise*

10. pagan
    (a) from Greek *poine*, "penalty"
    (b) from Old English *pearroc*, "enclosure"
    (c) from Latin *paganus*, "peasant"

---

Correct answers: 1 (c), 2 (a), 3 (a), 4 (a), 5 (b), 6 (c), 7 (b), 8 (a), 9 (a), 10 (c)

Your score: _____
(10–9 correct: superb; 8–6 correct: good; 5–4 correct: fair)

# Catching Up with Sophomore

## by Donald B. Sands

My favorite pejorative etymology:

I refer to our American substantive *sophomore*. The British English equivalent died out. The *Oxford English Dictionary* (*OED*) enters only two citations—1688 "...Sophy Moores..." and 1795 "...A Soph Mor..." The sense for this is "A student of the second year...At Cambridge *Obs*." What follows in the *OED* is completely American. Given are seven citations with the spelling *sophomore* (the first 1726, the last 1892) and three citations with the spelling *sophimore* (the first 1764, the last 1804). The *OED* etymology is all right for the obsolete British English form—namely, from Middle English *sophom*, "sophism."

Reading through the American citations in the *OED*, you find that all (except one) are related to academic classification and the majority seem to relate to early New England colleges, specifically Dartmouth and Harvard. In the late eighteenth and early nineteenth centuries, such places were devoted to Latin and Greek language learning. Greek certainly—the *New Testament* appeared in Greek, and such colleges specialized in the education of future clerics.

Unfortunately, *sophomore* somehow has retained its late seventeenth-century British English meaning—"a second-year student." But note that the pejorative adjective *sophomoric* (labeled "Chiefly *U.S.*" in the *OED*) came in early in American English, the first citation being 1837 in the *OED*, but 1813 in Mathews' *A Dictionary of Americanisms*. The equally pejorative *sophomorical* (and its adverbial form) the *OED* labels "*U.S.*" and gives a first citation dated 1847, while Mathews gives a first citation dated 1813.

Now, the *OED* enters as its headword *sophomore* just because it is the current form—the current American form, and this does not go back to a Middle English *sophom*. The ultima *-more* is an American creation. In all probability, the Greek-minded students at Yale, Harvard, and Dartmouth saw *sophos* in the first syllable and waggishly added a modification of *morós*, "foolish", namely, *-more*. Hence, the original late-eighteenth- and early-nineteenth-century New England academic connotation of *sophomore* was "educated fool." The two adjectival and pejorative derivatives clinch such a conclusion!

Who agrees with me here? Both the 1934 and the 1961 editions of Merriam's *International Dictionary* agree with me, as do most of the "college" or "desk" dictionaries. (See *Webster's New World Dictionary* of 1979, *Webster's New Collegiate Dictionary* of 1975, *Random House College Dictionary* of 1980.) The matter, however, is not hard and fast, unfortunately. *The American Heritage Dictionary: New College Edition* of 1981 indicates that *sophomore* is "Probably from earlier *sophumer*, arguments..." and *The American College Dictionary* of 1966 says essentially the same. But the most exhaustive etymological statement in an English-language dictionary is that in Vol. IX (page 5773) of the *Century Dictionary and Cyclopedia* of 1911. This, I note, starts off with the remark "Formerly *sophimore*, the altered form *sophomore* being made to simulate a formation [of the Greek wise + silly, foolish], as if in allusion to the exaggerated opinion that students at this age are apt to have of their wisdom...." I have not heard or read *sophomoron*, but expect I shall some day. And I do think that there are people astute enough to hear in the etymological overtones of the substantive *sophomore* a distant echo "educated fool." German has its *Bildungsphilister*—we have something similar in *sophomore*, similar, but much more subtle!

*Dr. Sands is Professor of English at the University of Michigan.*

# Chapter XVI

## Vocabulary Test No. 46

Which word or phrase is nearest in meaning to each of the following headwords?

1. **sapient** (sā′pē·ənt)
   - (a) dumb
   - (b) wise and discerning
   - (c) silly or foolish
   - (d) derisive

2. **nugatory** (nōō′gətōr′ē)
   - (a) of no value or significance
   - (b) golden
   - (c) obnoxious
   - (d) passing periodically from one region or climate to another, as certain birds

3. **megalomania** (meg′əlōmā′nē·ə)
   - (a) huge man-made structure
   - (b) one million deaths (a unit of hypothetical casualties in a nuclear war)
   - (c) lengthy account or explanation
   - (d) mental illness marked by delusions of greatness

4. **diffident** (dif′idənt)
   - (a) widely spread or scattered
   - (b) lacking confidence in oneself
   - (c) hard to deal with
   - (d) discursive or wordy

5. gullible   (gul'əbəl)
   (a)  easily swallowed
   (b)  like a sea bird
   (c)  easily deceived or cheated
   (d)  copious


6. erudition   (er'yŏŏdish'ən)
   (a)  profound learning acquired by study
   (b)  preciousness
   (c)  belch
   (d)  substitute, esp. of inferior quality


7. cognition   (kog·nish'ən)
   (a)  act or process of knowing or perceiving
   (b)  anger
   (c)  smokeless explosive powder composed of nitro-
        glycerin, cellulose nitrate, and petrolatum
   (d)  chief executive's prerogative


8. aphorism   (af'əriz'əm)
   (a)  malicious or damaging statement
   (b)  loss of the faculty of using or understanding lan-
        guage
   (c)  terse saying embodying a general truth
   (d)  the sign ('), used to indicate omission


9. savant   (savänt')
   (a)  grassy plain with low, scattered trees
   (b)  person of profound learning
   (c)  person with an IQ between 65 and 95
   (d)  person with vaulting ambition


10. moonshee   (mŏŏn'shē)
    (a)  native interpreter or language instructor
    (b)  illegally made liquor
    (c)  form of lunacy
    (d)  exploratory walk by an astronaut on the Moon's sur-
         face

236

**Correct answers:** 1 (b), 2 (a), 3 (d), 4 (b), 5 (c), 6 (a), 7 (a), 8 (c), 9 (b), 10 (a)

**Your score:** _____
(10–8 correct: superb; 7–5 correct: good; 4–3 correct: fair)

# Coiners of the Realm

Match these twenty-five words with their creators.

1. vitamin _____
2. cosmetology _____
3. calcium _____
4. ectoderm _____
5. bazooka _____
6. geriatrics _____
7. neutron _____
8. ecdysiast _____
9. iodine _____
10. overtone _____
11. financial _____
12. kind-hearted _____
13. decorous _____
14. entropy _____
15. aspirin _____
16. animism _____
17. Kodak _____
18. bromine _____
19. cirrhosis _____
20. stratosphere _____
21. jumbo _____
22. astigmatism _____
23. pantheist _____
24. geotropism _____
25. certitude _____

(a) was coined by the German scientist H. L. F. von Helmholtz (1821–94).

(b) was originally the name of a wind instrument that was invented and named by the American comedian Bob Burns (who died in 1956).

(c) was coined by the British statesman Edmund Burke (1729–97).

(d) was introduced by the English Bible translator Miles Coverdale (1488–1569)—along with many other terms such as "bloodguilty" and "loving-kindness."

(e) was first used at a dermatology conference in Budapest in 1935, by Dr. Aurel Voina.

(f) was coined, in 1890, as a trademark, by the

American inventor George Eastman (1854–1932).

(g) was coined in 1914 by I. L. Nascher (1863–1944), from Greek words for "old man" and "healing."

(h) was coined by the German physicist and chemist Georg Ernst Stahl (1660–1734).

(i) was coined to refer to a stripteaser by the American editor and satirist H. L. Mencken (1880–1956). It is, appropriately, a take-off, from a psychological term meaning a morbid impulse to disrobe in public, from a Greek word meaning "shedding, getting out of."

(j) was coined by the English philosopher Henry More (1614–87).

(k) was coined by the French meteorologist L. P. Teisserenc de Bort (1855–1913).

(l) was discovered and probably named in 1932 by the English physicist James Chadwig (born 1891).

(m) was coined by the English chemist Sir Humphrey Davy (1788–1829), from Latin for "lime."

(n) was coined in 1705 by the Irish deist John Toland (1670–1722).

(o) was introduced in the fourteenth century by Nicole Oresme, bishop of Lisieux in France.

(p) is derived from the name of a very large elephant exhibited by P. T. Barnum (1810–91).

(q) was coined by the French physician R. T. H. Laennec (1781–1826), from the Greek for "orange tawny," because of the yellowish color of the diseased liver.

(r) was coined in 1819 by the English mathematician and philosopher William Whewell (1794–1866).

(s) was coined in 1868 by the German botanist A. B. Frank (1839–1900).

(t) was named in 1811 by the French chemist Bernard Courtois (1777–1838), from Greek *ion*, "violet"; the English word was introduced by Sir Humphrey Davy (1778–1829).

(u) was first used in 1850 by the German physicist R. J. Clausius (1822–88).

(v) was coined by the French chemist Antoine Jérôme Balard (1802–76), from the Greek for "noisome smell."

(w) was coined in 1913 by the Polish biochemist Casimir Funk (born 1884), from the Latin for "life," plus "amine."

(x) was coined by H. Dreser in 1899.

(y) was coined by the German physician Robert Remak (1815–65).

---

Correct answers: 1 (w), 2 (e), 3 (m), 4 (y), 5 (b), 6 (g), 7 (l), 8 (i), 9 (t), 10 (a), 11 (c), 12 (d), 13 (j), 14 (u), 15 (x), 16 (h), 17 (f), 18 (v), 19 (q), 20 (k), 21 (p), 22 (r), 23 (n), 24 (s), 25 (o)

Your score: _____
(25–21 correct: superb; 20–16 correct: good; 15–11 correct: fair)

# Vocabulary Test No. 47

Which word or phrase is nearest in meaning to each of the following headwords?

1. **capitation** (kap'itā'shən)
   (a) transport of prisoners to the guillotine
   (b) tax levied against each person
   (c) alcove that leads directly into a governor's office
   (d) relationship between the parents of the groom and the parents of the bride

2. **pantheism** (pan'thē·iz'əm)
   (a) the belief that wood nymphs dictate weather patterns
   (b) the belief that the panther is really the king of the jungle
   (c) critical comment that closes a Broadway drama after one performance
   (d) philosophical doctrine that identifies God with the universe

3. **doyen** (doi·en')
   (a) dean
   (b) closest relative of the newt
   (c) lover of the Empress Dowager
   (d) second fiddle in an orchestra of more than sixty-seven players

4. **precursor** (prikûr'sər)
   (a) last word spoken before a child's first epithet
   (b) person or thing that precedes, as in a job or a method
   (c) route between Scylla and Charybdis
   (d) foreleg of a large dog

5. **votive** (vō'tiv)
   (a) breaking a deadlock in the election of a Pope

(b) done or given with or as a result of a vow
   (c) pertaining to the brace of candles on the cover of a copy of the Torah
   (d) lowered into the grave

6. artifice   (är'təfis)
   (a) expert in pre-Raphaelite color schemes
   (b) clever stratagem
   (c) skating rink without ice
   (d) award to a tyro watercolorist

7. malefic   (məlef'ik)
   (a) with a pastoral subject
   (b) horrendously seasick
   (c) meteorlike
   (d) producing evil

8. cupidity   (kyo͞opid'itē)
   (a) neck-gland secretion that can cause dwarfism
   (b) eager or inordinate desire, esp. for wealth
   (c) the most intimate act of love
   (d) emotion felt by many men on seeing lasciviousness

9. sedulous   (sej'ələs)
   (a) persevering
   (b) upright
   (c) reversing the direction, as of electrical current
   (d) metallic

10. ineffable   (inef'əbəl)
   (a) timid
   (b) oppressed or coerced
   (c) inefficient
   (d) unspeakable

---

Correct answers: 1 (b), 2 (d), 3 (a), 4 (b), 5 (b), 6 (b), 7 (d), 8 (b), 9 (a), 10 (d)

Your score: _____
(10–8 correct: superb; 7–5 correct: good; 4–3 correct: fair)

# Fill In the Blanks

Example:
an awkward, clumsy youth:
h o __ __ __ __ d e h __ __

The answer is "hobbledehoy."

1. a lengthy explanation or account: m __ g __ l l __ h
2. a confused mixture or medley: __ __ __ a n g e
3. a bird that feeds on insects captured in the air:
   __ __ __ __ __ t c h __ __
4. a showy, useless trifle: __ __ m c r __ __ k
5. forecastle: __ __ ' c ' s ' __ e
6. affected behavior or speech done for effect:
   h __ __ t r i __ n __ c s
7. an agent or act of retribution: __ e __ e s __ s
8. (in India) a person held in the highest esteem for his
   wisdom and saintliness: __ __ h a t __ __
9. a climbing shrub with showy clusters of flowers:
   w __ __ t e __ __ __
10. a loose, colorful pullover shirt for men, originally worn
    mainly in western Africa: __ a s h __ k __

---

Correct answers: 1. megillah 2. melange 3. flycatcher 4. gim-
crack 5. fo'c's'le 6. histrionics 7. nemesis 8. mahatma 9.
wisteria 10. dashiki

Your score: _____
(10–9 correct: superb; 8–6 correct: good; 5–4 correct: fair)

# Vocabulary Test No. 48

Which word or phrase is nearest in meaning to each of the following headwords from the poetry of T. S. Eliot?

1. **nocturne** (nok'tûrn)
   (a) night time
   (b) sparrow that flies only in the dark
   (c) knight in shining amor
   (d) musical composition appropriate to the night or evening

2. **marmoset** (mär'məzet')
   (a) tidal wave created by a typhoon
   (b) small South and Central American monkey resembling a squirrel
   (c) marble
   (d) product model or type, as of a sports car

3. **to supplicate** (sup'ləkāt')
   (a) to make a humble, earnest entreaty, esp. by prayer
   (b) to give the last meal, as to a condemned prisoner
   (c) to replace (one thing) by something else
   (d) to insure against loss or damage

4. **maculate** (mak'yəlit)
   (a) marked by a lofty or grandiose style
   (b) pertaining to the horizon created by the setting sun in the northern hemisphere
   (c) stained or spotted
   (d) strong and virile

5. **periphrasis** (pərif'rəsis)
   (a) rich-flavored tobacco favored by Scots
   (b) unnecessarily long and roundabout style of expression

    (c)  area between the anus and the genitals
    (d)  decay or destruction

6. **gullet** (gul′it)
    (a)  channel through which rain water runs
    (b)  jaw of a large-mouthed seabird
    (c)  esophagus, or throat or pharynx
    (d)  the pickoff move of a pitcher to second base

7. **polymath** (pol′ēmath′)
    (a)  female professor of mathematics
    (b)  person learned in many fields
    (c)  nitwit
    (d)  multicolored cube

8. **multifoliate** (mul′təfō′lē·it)
    (a)  in a dying state
    (b)  capable of moving spontaneously
    (c)  motivated
    (d)  having many leaves

9. **anfractuous** (anfrak′choo·əs)
    (a)  with both arms in slings
    (b)  near a roadbed on which railroad trackage rests
    (c)  sinuous
    (d)  gloomily or sullenly ill-humored

10. **maisonette** (mā′zənet′)
    (a)  kingdom into which the Lord entered
    (b)  block of marble or granite on which a sculpted figure sits
    (c)  dance floor in a nightclub
    (d)  small apartment (chiefly British)

---

Correct answers: 1 (d), 2 (b), 3 (a), 4 (c), 5 (b), 6 (c), 7 (b), 8 (d), 9 (c), 10 (d)

Your score:_____
(10–8 correct: superb; 7–5 correct: good; 4–3 correct: fair)

# Word Roots, Test P

Each of the following ten words stems from one of the three sources shown. Mark the correct answer.

1. horde
   (a) from Mongol *orda*, "camp"
   (b) from Old English *hore*, "whore"
   (c) from *horse* or *horseman*

2. dump
   (a) from German *dumm*, "stupid"
   (b) from Icelandic *dumpa*, "to thump"
   (c) from Latin *dum spiro, spero*, "while I breathe, I hope"

3. couch
   (a) from French *cotillion*, "petticoat"
   (b) from Latin *comes*, "companion of the king"
   (c) from Middle French *coucher*, "to lie down"

4. amnesty
   (a) from Middle French *amortir*, "to deaden"
   (b) from Latin *munitio*, "fortification"
   (c) from Greek *amnestia*, "forgetfulness"

5. coil
   (a) from Middle French *coillir*, "to collect"
   (b) from Arabic *kohl* (powder that darkens the eyelids)
   (c) from Greek *kaulos*, "stalk"

6. chauffeur
   (a) from Italian *ciarlatano*, "chatterer"
   (b) French *chauffer* for "stoker"
   (c) from Hebrew *shophar* (ram's horn blown as a wind instrument)

7. **to acquiesce**
   (a) from Latin *acquiescere*, "to rest"
   (b) from Late Latin *accognoscere*, "to know perfectly"
   (c) from Latin *acumen*, "sharpness"

8. **enormous**
   (a) from French *ennui*, "listlessness"
   (b) from Latin *norma*, "carpenter's square"
   (c) from Middle French *enorme*, "huge"

9. **minion**
   (a) from *Minyas*, the mythical Greek king of Orchomenus
   (b) from Middle French *mignon*, "darling"
   (c) from Latin *minister*, "servant"

10. **obdurate**
   (a) from Latin *obduratus*, "hardened"
   (b) a coined word, of unknown derivation, meaning impenitently wicked
   (c) from Greek *obeliskos*, "small spit"

---

Correct answers: 1 (a), 2 (b), 3 (c), 4 (c), 5 (a), 6 (b), 7 (a), 8 (c), 9 (b), 10 (a)

Your score: _____
(10–9 correct: superb; 8–6 correct: good; 5–4 correct: fair)

# It's Not What It May Sound Like

### by Jessica Julian

1. *Nosology* is the branch of medicine that deals with the classification of diseases (from Greek *nosos*, "disease"—unrelated to Latin *nasus*, from which comes our "nose").

2. The terms *nuclear complex*—a central conflict that is rooted in childhood—and *nuclear schizophrenia*—namely, process schizophrenia, as different from reactive schizophrenia—have nothing whatsoever to do with worries about radiation. (However, the term *nuclear neurosis* does refer to patterns of complaints found among individuals who live or work near nuclear electric-power plants.)

3. *Satellitosis* is an accumulation of neuroglia cells that forms around a damaged nerve cell—surrounding it like satellites (unrelated to an anxious concern over our Earth's natural or artificial satellites).

4. *Autosymbolism* is (according to the *Encyclopedia of Psychoanalysis*, by Eidelberg) "the direct transformation of abstract dream-content into concrete pictures that can be observed in the dream itself" (with no reference to Detroit).

5. A *Schick test* is a test for diphtheria in children (developed by Dr. Bela Schick—unrelated to the razor-blade manufacturer).

6. A *Dick test* is a skin test for scarlet fever (developed by Dr. George H. Dick and his wife, Dr. Gladys H. Dick).

7. The *fornicate gyrus* is an arched (*fornicatus* in Latin) or horseshoe-shaped prominence on the cerebral cortex between the hippocampal and cingulate gyri.

8. *Pilo-erection* is, literally, an erection of the hair (*pilus* in Latin), thus the temporary roughness of the skin

that is caused by sensations such as cold, fear, or sexual excitation—also called goose bumps, goose flesh, goose pimples, or goose skin.

9. A *Coxsackie infection* is a virus infection responsible for a wide range of diseases, such as respiratory ailments, aseptic meningitis, and paralytic disease. The name was derived from Coxsackie, New York, where the virus was first observed.

10. *Christmas disease* is a hereditary bleeding disease similar to hemophilia and was named after the first patient who was studied in detail, a Mr. Christmas (thus has no relation to the holiday or to Christ's wounds).

*Ms. Julian has contributed to a variety of media, including the CBS record* The Medium is the Massage.

# Chapter XVII

## Vocabulary Test No. 49

Which word or phrase is nearest in meaning to each of the following headwords, which might stump even a Mensaite?

1. panjandrum (panjan′drəm)
   (a) commercial-flight route, esp. northeast of Korea
   (b) self-important or pretentious official
   (c) music made by a lascivious woodland deity
   (d) subordinate ruler, often a despotic one

2. dithyramb (dith′əram′)
   (a) poem or other composition with wild and irregular form
   (b) whirlpool bath
   (c) state of flustered excitement
   (d) lack of unity or accord

3. rubicund (rōō′bəkund′)
   (a) unnaturally red or reddish, as the complexion
   (b) Caesar-like
   (c) unsophisticated country person
   (d) title or heading in an early manuscript or book, written or printed in red

4. spume (spyōōm)
   (a) mature male reproductive cell
   (b) ejected ballast

- (c)  band of muscle that encircles an orifice of the body
- (d)  foam, esp. tossed up by sea waves

5. apiary   (ā′pē·er′ē)
   - (a)  copycat
   - (b)  an opening, as a hole or slit
   - (c)  ideal
   - (d)  place in which bees are kept

6. sophism   (sof′izəm)
   - (a)  attitude of a second-year college student
   - (b)  clever but specious argument
   - (c)  tendency to fall asleep
   - (d)  morally ignoble or base interference

7. soporific   (sop′ərif′ik)
   - (a)  tending to cause sleep
   - (b)  grouchy
   - (c)  chronically drunk
   - (d)  complex or intricate

8. rapacious   (rəpā′shəs)
   - (a)  moving swiftly toward a goal
   - (b)  speaking wildly and loudly
   - (c)  plundering or greedy
   - (d)  having succeeded in evading the penalty for a crime

9. labile   (lā′bil)
   - (a)  characterized by a brilliant change of colors
   - (b)  apt to change, esp. emotionally or chemically
   - (c)  with the lips
   - (d)  pertaining to laboratory experiments

10. to supervene   (sōō′pərvēn′)
    - (a)  to oversee (work or workers)
    - (b)  to occur as something extraneous or unexpected
    - (c)  to be written or printed high on a line of text, as a
           small letter or number
    - (d)  to lie on the back

Correct answers: 1 (b), 2 (a), 3 (a), 4 (d), 5 (d), 6 (b), 7 (a), 8 (c), 9 (b), 10 (b)

Your score: _____
(10–8 correct: superb; 7–5 correct: good; 4–3 correct: fair)

# Eponyms

The items at the left refer to proper names; the items at the right define words or phrases that are derived from these proper names. Match them.

Example:
an eighteenth-century judge_____ to hang or otherwise kill (a person) by mob action and without legal authority

The answer is "to lynch" (Charles Lynch, 1736–96).

1. an Irish town, former site of a fair _____

2. a French architect _____

3. an Austrian physicist _____

4. an English physician _____

5. a county in England _____

6. a city in Italy _____

7. a Russian statesman _____

8. a U.S. chemist _____

9. a hunting center in England _____

10. a hotel in Manhattan _____

(a) an elaborate display that conceals something shabby or unpleasant

(b) a thick wool fabric with a short nap

(c) a salad of celery, diced apples, nuts, and mayonnaise

(d) a change in the frequency with which waves (such as sound or light) reach an observer when the source and the observer are in rapid motion with respect to each other

(e) a colorless or brown blistering poison gas used in chemical warfare

(f) a wild, noisy fight

(g) a roof with four sides, each with two slopes, the lower one steep, the upper one nearly flat

(h) pertaining to a period of the Paleozoic era, characterized by the advent of amphibians

(i) one of a Mediterranean breed of chickens that are prolific layers of white-shelled eggs

(j) a disease characterized by progressive chronic inflammation and enlargement of the lymph nodes

---

Correct answers: 1 (f) donnybrook (Donnybrook), 2 (g) mansard (François Mansart, 1598–1666), 3 (d) Doppler effect (Christian J. Doppler, 1803–53), 4 (j) Hodgkin's disease (Thomas Hodgkin, 1798–1866), 5 (h) Devonian (Devon), 6 (i) leghorn (Livorno, in English Leghorn), 7 (a) Potemkin village (unjustly named for Grigori A. Potemkin, 1739–91), 8 (e) lewisite (W. L. Lewis, 1878–1943), 9 (b) melton (Melton Mowbray), 10 (c) Waldorf salad (Waldorf-Astoria Hotel)

Your score: _____
(10–9 correct; superb; 8–6 correct: good; 5–4 correct: fair)

# Vocabulary Test No. 50

Which word or phrase is nearest in meaning to each of the following headwords?

1. lachrymose (lak'rəmōs')
   (a) given to shedding tears
   (b) deficient or absent
   (c) without vigor, interest, or enthusiasm
   (d) liveried

2. pusillanimous (pyoo͞'sələn'əməs)
   (a) lacking courage or resolution
   (b) obnoxiously self-assertive
   (c) becoming putrid
   (d) pure, virginal

3. mendacious (mendā'shəs)
   (a) useless
   (b) habitually speaking the truth
   (c) addicted to telling lies
   (d) usable

4. flaccid (flak'sid)
   (a) slender and erect
   (b) soft and limp
   (c) narrow
   (d) overcome with bewilderment

5. bombast (bom'bast)
   (a) explosive outburst
   (b) vigorous attack
   (c) pretentious, pompous language
   (d) round mass of medicine, larger than an ordinary pill

256

6. **termagant** (tûr′məgənt)
   (a) word or group of words designating something, esp. in a particular field
   (b) definite end or boundary
   (c) tropical, social insect highly destructive to wooden buildings
   (d) violent, brawling woman

7. **febrile** (fē′brəl)
   (a) physically weak, as from age
   (b) lacking normal mental powers
   (c) pertaining to or marked by fever
   (d) self-destructive

8. **to gainsay** (gān′sā′)
   (a) to advance rapidly, on the wings of speech
   (b) to deny
   (c) to state something cheerfully
   (d) to produce profit at every turn

9. **pariah** (pərī′ə)
   (a) county (in Louisiana)
   (b) hooded fur coat for wear in arctic regions
   (c) social outcast
   (d) dessert made of layers of ice cream, fruit, and syrup

10. **oxymoron** (ok′simōr′on)
    (a) member of the bovine family
    (b) figure of speech that combines two or more contradictory ideas
    (c) oxygen enrichment
    (d) low shoe laced over the instep, popular among English university lads

---

Correct answers: 1 (a), 2 (a), 3 (c), 4 (b), 5 (c), 6 (d), 7 (c), 8 (b), 9 (c), 10 (b)

Your score: _____
(10–8 correct: superb; 7–5 correct: good; 4–3 correct: fair)

## There *Is* a Word for It

Example:
to be fretfully discontented:
r _____

The answer is to "repine."

1. having many curves, bends, or turns:
   s _____

2. a small tea cake, variously frosted and decorated:
   p _____ f _____

3. a shackle for the hands or feet:
   m _____

4. a nickname, esp. one with a special association:
   s _____

5. a flat sandal, usually with a canvas upper:
   e _____

6. a long clifflike ridge of land or rock:
   e _____

7. dry food for livestock: p _____

8. (in Spain and Portugal) an older woman serving as chaperon of a young lady: d _____

9. an alcoholic liquor made by fermenting honey and water:
   m _____

10. a group of subordinates or attendants of a high-ranking person: r _____

Correct answers: 1. sinuous 2. petit four 3. manacle 4. sobriquet 5. espadrille 6. escarpment 7. provender 8. duenna (dueña) 9. mead 10. retinue

Your score:_____
(10–9 correct: superb; 8–6 correct: good; 5–4 correct: fair)

# Vocabulary Test No. 51

Which word or phrase is nearest in meaning to each of the following headwords, which can be described as grandiloquent?

1. scabrous (skab′rəs)
   (a) bearing inscriptions (as a stone coffin)
   (b) pertaining to a sheath for a sword or dagger
   (c) indecent or obscene
   (d) honoring a large, dark-shelled beetle, regarded as sacred by the ancient Egyptians

2. mordant (môr′dᵊnt)
   (a) drawing one's last breath
   (b) caustic or sarcastic, as in expression
   (c) suggesting an unhealthy mental state
   (d) pertaining to edible mushrooms having spongy caps

3. defenestration (dēfen′istrā′shen)
   (a) the act of throwing a person or thing out of a window
   (b) design and disposition of windows and other exterior openings of a building
   (c) line of strikers or other demonstrators serving as pickets
   (d) shell of a submarine

4. morganatic (môr′gənat′ik)
   (a) pertaining to a form of marriage between a man of high rank and a woman of lower station
   (b) payable at the end of the year by Wall Street brokers
   (c) temporarily inactive
   (d) living in tropical waters

5. empyreal (empir′ē·əl)
   (a) having nothing in the hands
   (b) pertaining to the highest heaven in the cosmology of the ancients

260

    (c)  accumulating in the eyes during sleep (namely, specks of "dust")

    (d)  pertaining to the tail assembly of an airplane or airship

6. **Procrustean** (prōkrus'te·ən)
   - (a) fecund
   - (b) tending to produce conformity by violent or arbitrary means
   - (c) dealing with the rectum and anus
   - (d) pertaining to the underside of a sea slug

7. **hobbledehoy** (hob'əldēhoi')
   - (a) donkey work
   - (b) extraordinary size or amount
   - (c) lame child at play
   - (d) awkward, clumsy youth

8. **avatar** (av'ətär')
   - (a) insatiable greed for riches
   - (b) avoirdupois
   - (c) embodiment or manifestation, as of a principle
   - (d) daydreaming about flying

9. **mulct** (mulkt)
   - (a) grass favored by cows in the Southwest
   - (b) offspring of a male donkey and a mare
   - (c) a fine, esp. for a misdemeanor
   - (d) thin, vertical bay, as between windowpanes

10. **threnody** (thren'ədē)
    - (a) group of three
    - (b) sudden, keen excitement
    - (c) song of lamentation
    - (d) great number of persons or things crowded or considered together

---

Correct answers: 1 (c), 2 (b), 3 (a), 4 (a), 5 (b), 6 (b), 7 (d), 8 (c), 9 (c), 10 (c)

Your score:_____
(10–8 correct: superb; 7–5 correct: good; 4–3 correct: fair)

# Word Roots, Test Q

Each of the following ten words stems from one of the three sources shown. Mark the correct answer.

1. patrol
   - (a) from Latin *patiens*, "suffering"
   - (b) from Greek *patriotes*, "fellow countryman"
   - (c) from French *patrouiller*, originally "to tramp in the mud"

2. petulant
   - (a) from Latin *petulantia*, "impudence"
   - (b) from French *petun*, "tobacco"
   - (c) from Latin *pectus*, "breast"

3. recidivist
   - (a) from Latin *reciprocare*, "to move back and forth"
   - (b) from Latin *recidivus*, "relapsing"
   - (c) from Latin *recitare*, "to read aloud"

4. hussy
   - (a) from Dutch *husselen*, "to shake"
   - (b) from Old English *huswif*, "housewife"
   - (c) from Old Danish *husthing*, "house assembly"

5. parlor
   - (a) from *Parnassus* (mountain in Greece sacred to the Muses)
   - (b) from Old French *parler*, "to speak"
   - (c) from Middle English *parail*, "apparel"

6. pariah
   - (a) from Latin *paries*, "wall"
   - (b) from Tamil *paraiyan*, "one of low caste"
   - (c) from Greek *paroikia*, "neighborhood"

7. queue
   (a) from *Cuero*, a town in Texas
   (b) from Old English *cwicu*, "living"
   (c) from Old French *coe*, "tail"

8. ragamuffin
   (a) from Middle English *Ragamoffyn*, demon in the medieval poem *Piers Plowman*
   (b) from Lord *Raglan* (1788–1855)
   (c) from Arabic *rahat*, "palm of the hand"

9. shaggy
   (a) from Old French *seuwiere*, "sluice"
   (b) from Old English *sceacga*, "hair of the head"
   (c) from Old English *sceabb*, "scab"

10. to launder
    (a) from *La Vallière*, one of the mistresses of Louis XIV
    (b) from Middle French *lavandier*, "washerwoman"
    (c) from Middle English *lawnd*, "thin or sheer fabric"

---

Correct answers: 1 (c), 2 (a), 3 (b), 4 (b), 5 (b), 6 (b), 7 (c), 8 (a), 9 (b), 10 (b)

Your score:_____
(10–9 correct: superb; 8–6 correct: good; 5–4 correct: fair)

# A Dunce Cap for the Word Dunce

by Walter D. Glanze

Dictionaries tell us that a *dunce* is a dull-witted, ignorant person, or a slow and backward student, and that the word *dunce* comes from the name of John Duns Scotus, the thirteenth-century theologian and philosopher. What dictionaries do not tell us is the story of the great injustice we do him every time we say *dunce*.

Duns Scotus (who was born c. 1265, probably in the village of *Duns* in Scotland, and died on November 8, 1308, in Cologne, Germany) was one of the most influential thinkers of medieval Europe. Because of the great subtlety of his thoughts, he was given the name "Doctor Subtilis," and when his followers were called "Dunsmen," "Dunses," or "Dunces," it meant originally that they were thought of as very learned men. But his scholastic system, Scotism, was in conflict with Thomism, the system of Saint Thomas Aquinas (c. 1225–74), and soon the Thomists ridiculed Duns Scotus and his followers as *dunces* in the modern, derogatory sense. The smear campaign was successful and the reversed meaning became popular, perhaps because people could not understand the subtlety of the Dunsmen's thoughts the way they would not understand the babbling of a moron. Even the sixteenth-century Humanists—who should have known better—later used the word *dunce* when referring to what they saw as the "useless" subtlety of the Scotists.

The real irony is that while Thomas still tried to make faith and intellect compatible, Duns Scotus tried to establish *the limits and therefore the separate identity* of rational thought (as clearly different from the body as well as from divine revelation), and it was his method that eventually drove a wedge between philosophy and religion, freeing philosophy from its dependence on Christian theology. Duns Scotus did not really intend this development; yet, in a way, this independent and courageous thinker should rightfully occupy a place in history as the granddaddy or patron saint of free inquiry, of the primacy of intelligence over conventional truth and acquired knowledge—quite the opposite of a *dunce*.

We can't decree that a word should not be used anymore, or that it should henceforth be used in a different sense. But as for me—I'll never use the words *dunce, duncery, dunce cap, duncial,* or *duncish* again. (If I did, I'd feel like a—well, a dunce.)

*Mr. Glanze has edited English and foreign-language dictionaries as well as dictionaries of psychology and psychiatry, science, law, mass media and communication, music, poetry, medicine, and other fields.*

# Your Total Score

# Vocabulary Tests

**Vocabulary Tests, Nos. 1 to 51:**

| | | | | |
|---|---|---|---|---|
| 1 _____ | 11 _____ | 21 _____ | 31 _____ | 41 _____ |
| 2 _____ | 12 _____ | 22 _____ | 32 _____ | 42 _____ |
| 3 _____ | 13 _____ | 23 _____ | 33 _____ | 43 _____ |
| 4 _____ | 14 _____ | 24 _____ | 34 _____ | 44 _____ |
| 5 _____ | 15 _____ | 25 _____ | 35 _____ | 45 _____ |
| 6 _____ | 16 _____ | 26 _____ | 36 _____ | 46 _____ |
| 7 _____ | 17 _____ | 27 _____ | 37 _____ | 47 _____ |
| 8 _____ | 18 _____ | 28 _____ | 38 _____ | 48 _____ |
| 9 _____ | 19 _____ | 29 _____ | 39 _____ | 49 _____ |
| 10 _____ | 20 _____ | 30 _____ | 40 _____ | 50 _____ |
| | | | | 51 _____ |

**Subtotal for Vocabulary Tests, Nos. 1 to 51:_____**

(510–461 correct: superb; 460–306 correct: good; 305–200 correct: fair)

# Word Tests

**Word Roots, A to Q:**

| A ___ | E ___ | I ___ | L ___ | O ___ |
|-------|-------|-------|-------|-------|
| B ___ | F ___ | J ___ | M ___ | P ___ |
| C ___ | G ___ | K ___ | N ___ | Q ___ |
| D ___ | H ___ | | | |

**Subtotal for Word Roots, A to Q:** _____
(170–151 correct: superb; 150–101 correct: good; 100–65 correct: fair)

# Other Etymology Tests

**Eponyms:**

| chapter IV | _____ | chapter XIV | _____ |
|------------|--------|-------------|--------|
| chapter X | _____ | chapter XVII | _____ |

**Coiners of the Realm:**

| chapter VI | _____ | chapter XVI | _____ |
|------------|--------|-------------|--------|

**False Impressions:**

chapter I _____

**State the Name!**

chapter IX _____

**What We Do to Our Children:**

chapter XI _____

**In Words:**

chapter XV _____

**What Our Presidents Didn't Know:**

| chapter III | _____ | chapter XII | _____ |
|-------------|--------|-------------|--------|
| chapter VI | _____ | chapter XV | _____ |
| chapter IX | _____ | | |

**Subtotal for Other Etymology Tests:** _____

(238–201 correct: superb; 200–136 correct: good; 135–70 correct: fair)

## Miscellaneous Tests

Fill In the Blanks:

| | | | |
|---|---|---|---|
| chapter I | _____ | chapter X | _____ |
| chapter IV | _____ | chapter XIII | _____ |
| chapter VII | _____ | chapter XVI | _____ |

There *Is* a Word for It:

| | | | |
|---|---|---|---|
| chapter II | _____ | chapter XI | _____ |
| chapter V | _____ | chapter XIV | _____ |
| chapter VIII | _____ | chapter XVII | _____ |

Over There:

| | | | |
|---|---|---|---|
| chapter II | _____ | chapter XIII | _____ |

New Kids on the Block:

chapter VII _____

As We Weren't Saying:

chapter III _____

Scramblings:

| | | | |
|---|---|---|---|
| chapter V | _____ | chapter XII | _____ |
| chapter VIII | _____ | | |

Subtotal for Miscellaneous Tests: _____

(231–206 correct: superb; 205–146 correct: good; 145–105
correct: fair)

# Summary

Subtotals:

Vocabulary Tests, Nos. 1 to 51  _____
Word Roots, A to Q  _____
Word Tests  _____
Other Etymology Tests  _____
Miscellaneous Tests  _____

Your grand total:_____

(1,149–1,019 correct: superb; 1,018–689 correct: good; 688–440 correct: fair)

N.B. Besides mere addition, the ratings of subtotals and grand total include cumulative factors of difficulty.

# About the Author

Jerome Agel's thirty books include collaborations with Marshall McLuhan, Carl Sagan, Stanley Kubrick, Herman Kahn, R. Buckminster Fuller, Humphry Osmond, Isaac Asimov, and Allan Cott. His books include the novel *Deliverance in Shanghai* and the quiz books *America at Random* and *Sports at Random*. His three other Ballantine books are *Test Your Bible Power*, *The Radical Therapist*, and *Rough Times*.

# *Authoritative Guides to Better Self-Expression:*

**Available at your bookstore or use this coupon.**

____ **THE WORD-A-DAY VOCABULARY BUILDER,**
Berger Evans with Jess Stein (Ed.)        30610   2.50
In just five minutes a day anyone can enlarge his or her vocabulary and learn to speak and write more clearly and persuasively. Never before available in mass market paperback, this is an extremely effective guide to developing a technique that is natural, practical and habit forming! For students, professors, business people—everyone!

____ **1,000 MOST IMPORTANT WORDS,** Norman W. Schur       29863   3.50
Available for the first time in mass market paperback, this guide helps us unlock our "passive" vocabularies, and as we develop a keener appreciation of the richness of our language. Fun and easy to use!

____ **THE RANDOM HOUSE DICTIONARY,** Editor in Chief: Jess Stein    32293   3.95
Up to date and comprehensive, with more than 74,000 entries—including current business, scientific, and technical terms. Slang and idiomatic vocabulary. Numerous usage labels, notes, and example sentences. Valuable supplements include a Basic Manual of Style. Much more!

____ **THE RANDOM HOUSE BASIC SPELLER/DIVIDER,** Editor: Jess Stein   29255   2.95
More than 50,000 entries, more than any comparable book. Includes names of nations, states, famous people, lists of common abbreviations, and a Basic Manual of Style.

____ **THE RANDOM HOUSE BASIC DICTIONARY OF SYNONYMS AND ANTONYMS.**
Editor: Laurence Urdang                 29712   3.50
When the "nearly-right" word won't do, this handy volume provides over 80,000 synonyms and antonyms, with all entries easy to locate in one alphabetical listing.

**BB**   **BALLANTINE MAIL SALES**
       **Dept. TA, 201 E. 50th St., New York, N.Y. 10022**

Please send me the BALLANTINE or DEL REY BOOKS I have checked above. I am enclosing $...............(add $2.00 to cover postage and handling for the first book and 50¢ each additional book). Send check or money order—no cash or C.O.D.'s please. Prices are subject to change without notice. Valid in U.S. only. All orders are subject to availability of books.

Name_____

Address_____

City_____State_____Zip Code_____

03        Allow at least 4 weeks for delivery.     3/90     TA-46